D1346848

SPACE

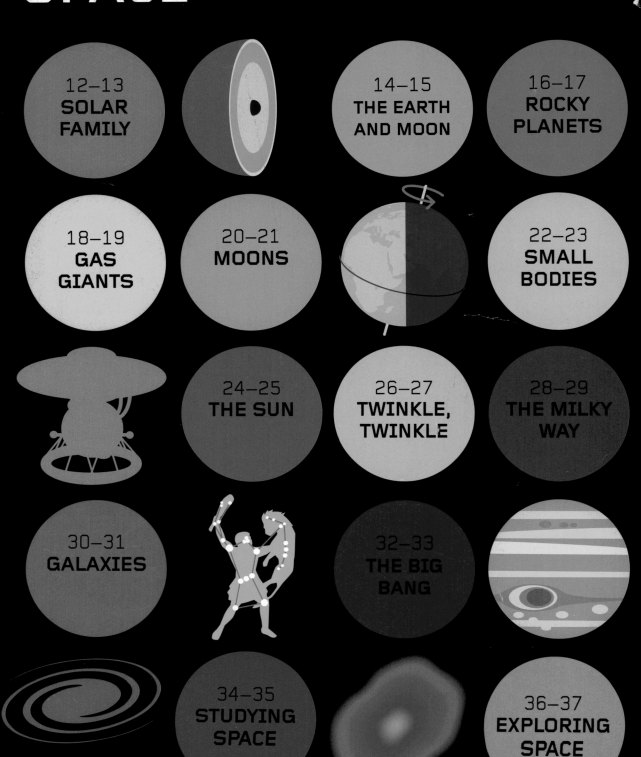

PLANET EARTH

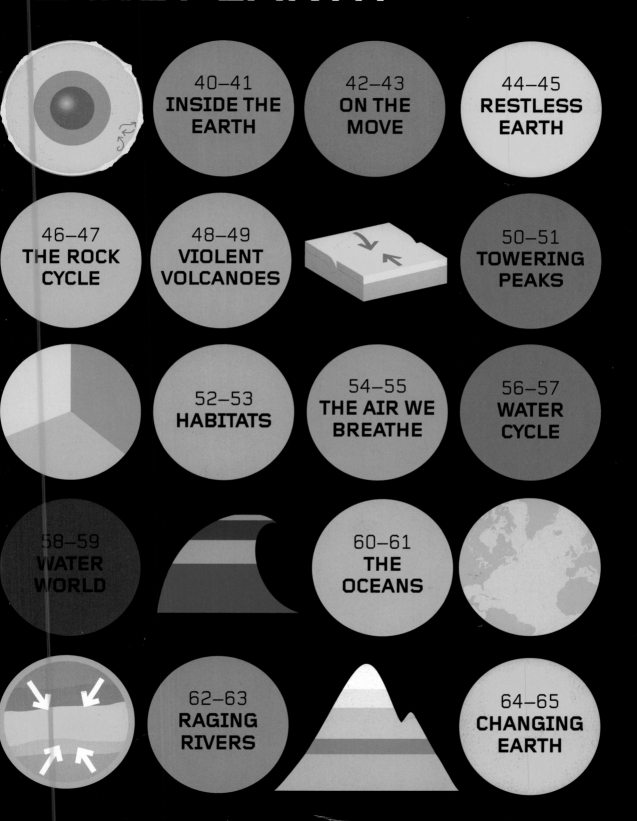

NATURAL RESOURCES

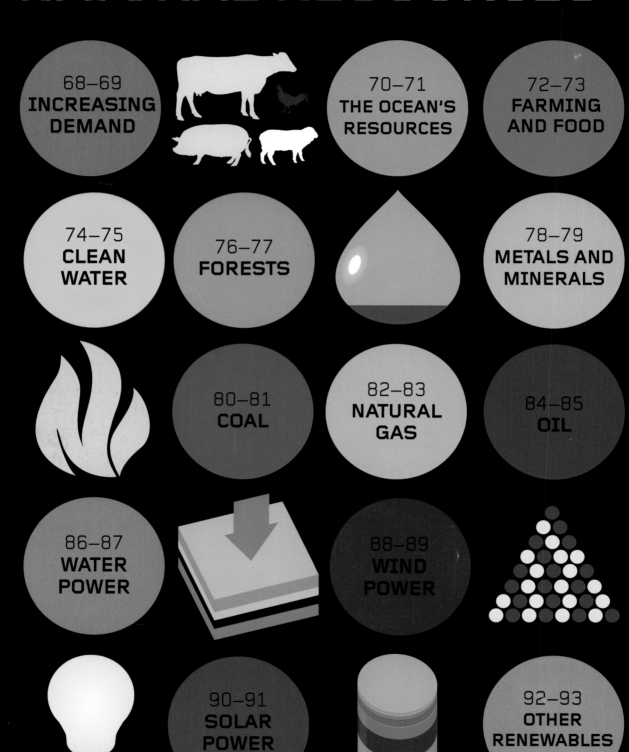

NATURAL WORLD

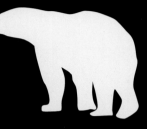
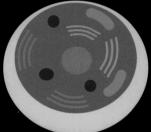
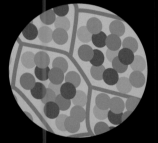

ANIMAL KINGDOM

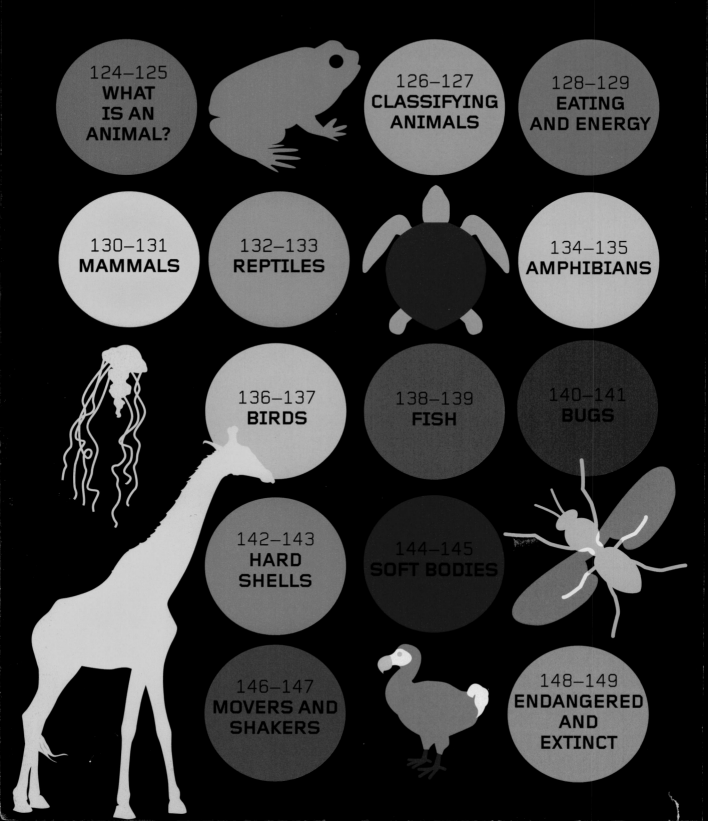

124–125
WHAT IS AN ANIMAL?

126–127
CLASSIFYING ANIMALS

128–129
EATING AND ENERGY

130–131
MAMMALS

132–133
REPTILES

134–135
AMPHIBIANS

136–137
BIRDS

138–139
FISH

140–141
BUGS

142–143
HARD SHELLS

144–145
SOFT BODIES

146–147
MOVERS AND SHAKERS

148–149
ENDANGERED AND EXTINCT

HUMAN BODY

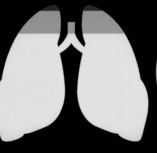
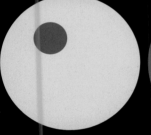

WELCOME TO THE WORLD OF INFOGRAPHICS

Using icons, graphics and pictograms, infographics visualise data and information in a whole new way!

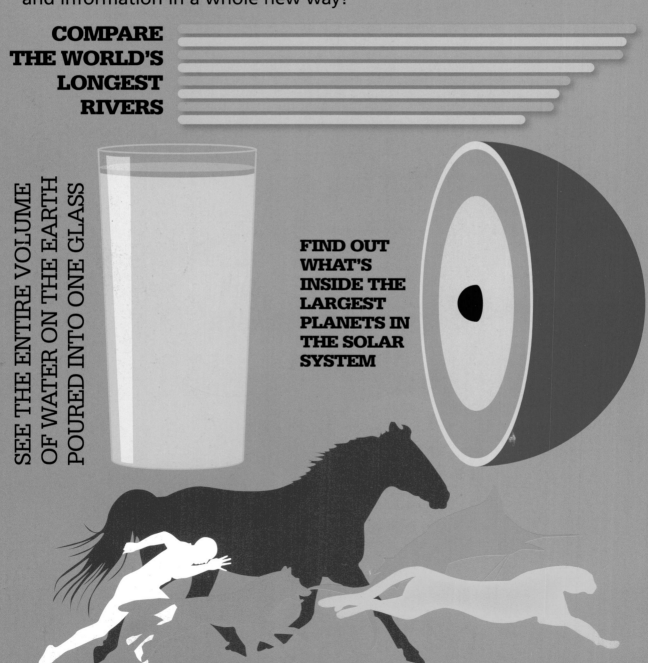

COMPARE THE WORLD'S LONGEST RIVERS

SEE THE ENTIRE VOLUME OF WATER ON THE EARTH POURED INTO ONE GLASS

FIND OUT WHAT'S INSIDE THE LARGEST PLANETS IN THE SOLAR SYSTEM

DISCOVER WHICH ANIMAL WOULD WIN THE GOLD MEDAL IN A SPRINT RACE

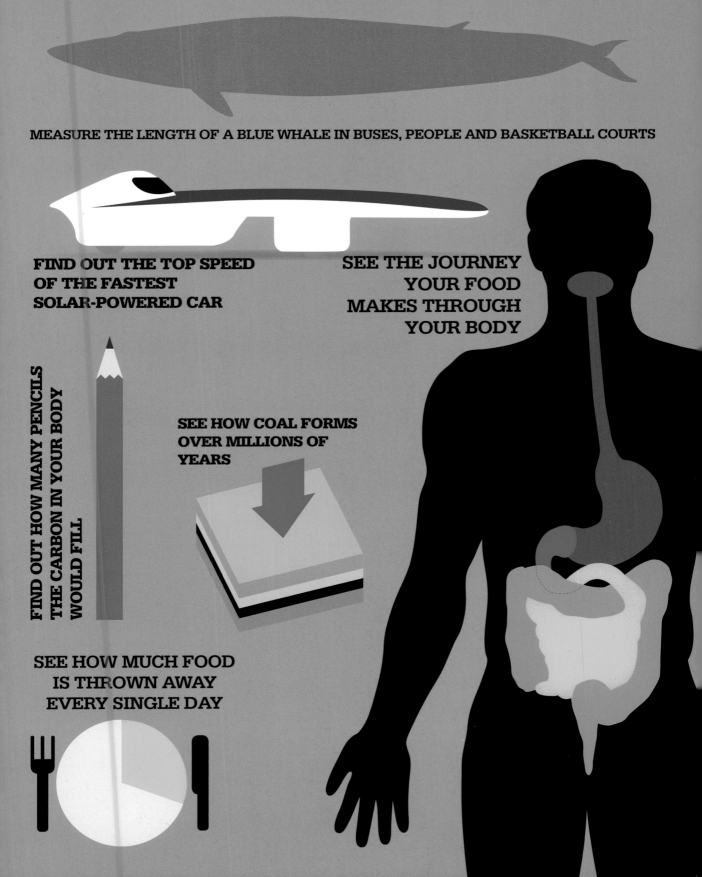

MEASURE THE LENGTH OF A BLUE WHALE IN BUSES, PEOPLE AND BASKETBALL COURTS

FIND OUT THE TOP SPEED
OF THE FASTEST
SOLAR-POWERED CAR

SEE THE JOURNEY
YOUR FOOD
MAKES THROUGH
YOUR BODY

FIND OUT HOW MANY PENCILS
THE CARBON IN YOUR BODY
WOULD FILL

SEE HOW COAL FORMS
OVER MILLIONS OF
YEARS

SEE HOW MUCH FOOD
IS THROWN AWAY
EVERY SINGLE DAY

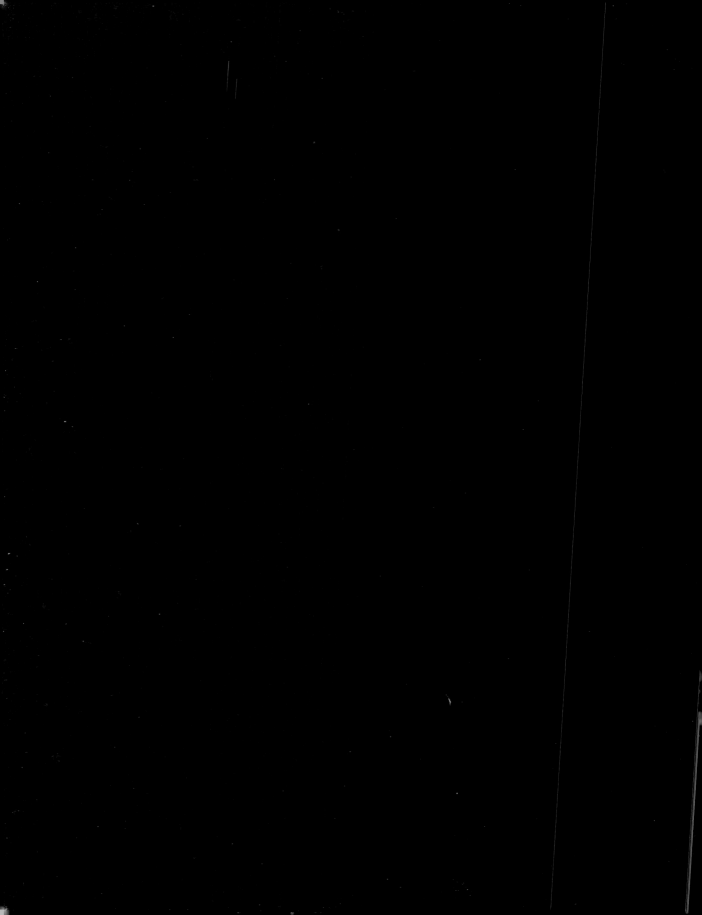

SOLAR FAMILY

At the centre of the Solar System is a huge ball of burning gas – the Sun. Spinning around this are eight planets, many dwarf planets and millions of small chunks of rock and ice.

THE SUN

is our nearest star and it measures 1.4 million kilometres across. It is the largest object in the Solar System, making up more than 99 per cent of the system's mass.

ROCKY PLANETS

The four planets that are nearest to the Sun are mostly made from rocks and metals.

MERCURY

VENUS

EARTH

MARS

330,000

The Sun has 330,000 times more mass than planet Earth.

MILLION KM FROM SUN

0   500

SUN
MERCURY
VENUS
EARTH
MARS
JUPITER

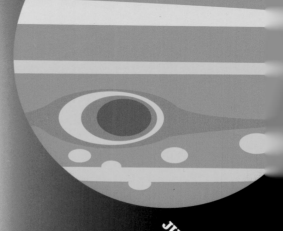

JUPITER

ORBITING DISTANCES

The planets go around the Sun in slightly oval-shaped orbits. This means that their distances from the Sun will vary at different points in their orbits.

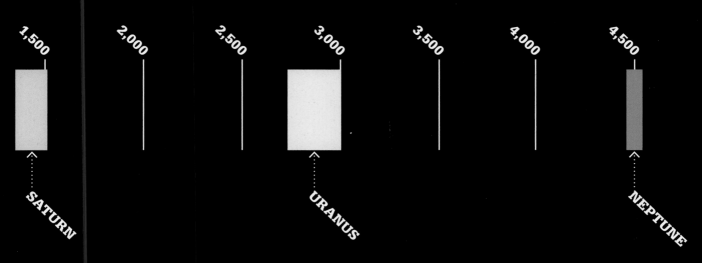

1,500   2,000   2,500   3,000   3,500   4,000   4,500

SATURN   URANUS   NEPTUNE

GAS GIANTS

The four planets that are farthest from the Sun are enormous balls of gas with solid balls of rocks and metals at their centres.

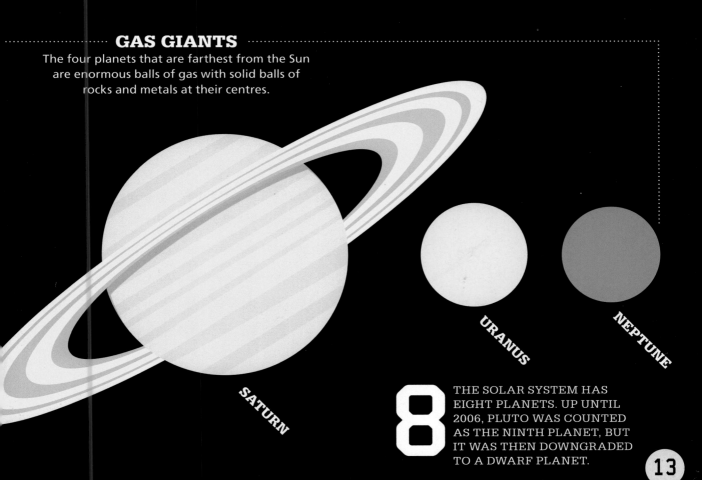

SATURN   URANUS   NEPTUNE

8 THE SOLAR SYSTEM HAS EIGHT PLANETS. UP UNTIL 2006, PLUTO WAS COUNTED AS THE NINTH PLANET, BUT IT WAS THEN DOWNGRADED TO A DWARF PLANET.

THE EARTH AND MOON

A year is the time it takes for a planet to go around the Sun. During its path around the Sun, the Earth is orbited by the Moon, which goes around the Earth every 27.3 days.

TIDES

The Moon's gravitational pull causes the water of the Earth's oceans to bulge, creating high tides in some areas and low tides in others. As the Earth rotates, the locations of high and low tides change.

23.45°

The angle of the Earth's tilt in relation to the Sun.

SUMMER IN NORTHERN HEMISPHERE

THE EARTH IS FARTHEST FROM THE SUN DURING JULY.

WINTER IN SOUTHERN HEMISPHERE

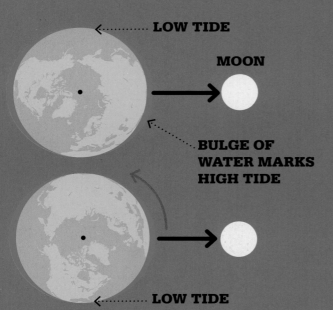

LOW TIDE

MOON

BULGE OF WATER MARKS HIGH TIDE

LOW TIDE

AN EARTH YEAR

At two points in its orbit, the Earth has 12 hours of day and 12 hours of night. These are called the equinoxes. The points where the lengths of a day or night are their longest are called the solstices.

384,400 KM

Distance from the Earth to the Moon.

30 EARTHS WOULD FIT BACK-TO-BACK IN THE DISTANCE BETWEEN THE EARTH AND THE MOON

NIGHT AND DAY

As the Earth spins around, one half of the planet points towards the Sun and experiences day. At the same time, the other half points away from the Sun and experiences night.

DAY **NIGHT**

Average orbital speed of the Earth around the Sun

107,200 KM/H

SEASONS

At different times of the year, some parts of the planet are tilted towards the Sun, while others are tilted away. The areas tilted towards the Sun experience summer, with long days and warm weather. Those tilted away from the Sun experience winter, with colder weather and shorter days.

SUN

WINTER IN NORTHERN HEMISPHERE

THE EARTH IS CLOSEST TO THE SUN DURING JANUARY

SUMMER IN SOUTHERN HEMISPHERE

EQUATOR

365.3 DAYS

The length of time it takes the Earth to complete one orbit around the Sun.

1 AU

To measure the very large distances around the Solar System, astronomers use astronomical units (AU). One astronomical unit is the distance from the Earth to the Sun, which is approximately

150 MILLION KM.

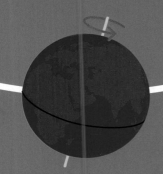

ROCKY PLANETS

The four planets nearest to the Sun (Mercury, Venus, Earth and Mars) are the smallest in the Solar System. However, these amazing worlds have towering peaks, poisonous atmospheres and surfaces that are both scorching hot and icy cold.

<...... **CRUST**

UNDER THE SURFACE

The outside of a rocky planet is surrounded by a hard, thin crust. Beneath this, the mantle is usually made from liquid rock. At the centre is a hard core made from metals, such as iron or nickel.

<.......... **METALLIC CORE**

<..................... **ROCKY MANTLE**

ATMOSPHERES

Three of the rocky planets have layers of gases around them called atmospheres. Mercury has an atmosphere, but it is very thin, compared to the other three.

EVEREST EARTH
8,848 M

VENUS FACTS

Atmospheric pressure is

92 TIMES

greater than that on Earth's surface.
That is the same as being

1 KILOMETRE

deep in the Earth's oceans –
more than enough to squash
a person flat. Its atmosphere has clouds of

SULPHURIC ACID

that are blown around at
speeds of 100 metres
per second.

MERCURY

TEMPERATURES ON MERCURY
RANGE FROM 427°C ON THE
SUN-FACING SIDE TO JUST
-183°C IN THE SHADE.

427°C

300°C

200°C

100°C
Boiling point
of water

57.8 °C
Highest recorded
temperature on Earth

37 °C
Human body temperature

15°C
Average surface
temperature on Earth

0°C

-89.2 °C
Lowest recorded
temperature on Earth

-100°C

-183°C

THE LARGEST VOLCANO IN THE SOLAR SYSTEM

OLYMPUS MONS
ON MARS IS 22,000 METRES
TALL. IT MEASURES
700 KM ACROSS
AND IS SURROUNDED
BY CLIFFS THAT ARE
10 KM HIGH.

OLYMPUS MONS IS

26.5

TIMES TALLER THAN THE **BURJ KHALIFA**, THE WORLD'S TALLEST BUILDING, WHICH MEASURES 830 M.

GAS GIANTS

These gigantic worlds do not have a solid surface. Instead, they are covered with swirling gases that have raging storms and the strongest winds in the Solar System.

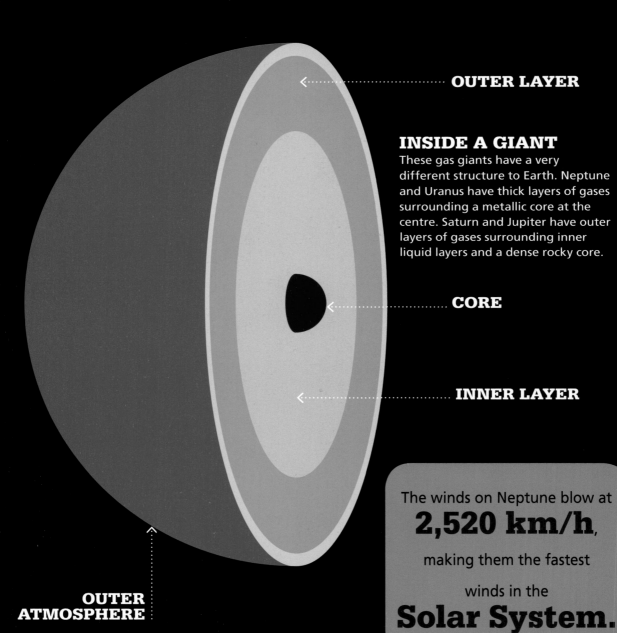

OUTER LAYER

INSIDE A GIANT
These gas giants have a very different structure to Earth. Neptune and Uranus have thick layers of gases surrounding a metallic core at the centre. Saturn and Jupiter have outer layers of gases surrounding inner liquid layers and a dense rocky core.

CORE

INNER LAYER

OUTER ATMOSPHERE

The winds on Neptune blow at

2,520 km/h,

making them the fastest

winds in the

Solar System.

GREAT RED SPOT

A powerful storm that's been raging on Jupiter, it is bigger than our planet and has lasted for nearly

350 YEARS

Winds inside the storm reach speeds of up to

432 KM/H

RINGS

All four gas giant planets have systems of rings around their equators. The most visible of these surround Saturn.

URANUS HAS
A TILT OF

98°

URANUS

JUPITER HAS A TILT OF 3.13°

SATURN HAS A TILT
OF 26.73°

NEPTUNE HAS A TILT
OF 28.32°

Saturn's rings stretch for hundreds of thousands of kilometres, but they are only about 10 metres thick. The rings are made up of particles which range in size from specks of dust to

10 METRES

in diameter – bigger than an
African elephant.

MOONS

Moons are natural satellites that orbit other bodies. Six of the eight planets in the Solar System have their own moon systems. These moons have frozen seas and explosive volcanoes.

300 KM

COMPARISON OF THE BIGGEST MOONS

GANYMEDE
JUPITER
5,262 KM

TITAN
SATURN
5,152 KM

CALLISTO
JUPITER
4,821 KM

MOON
EARTH
3,476 KM

ICE CRUST

Europa (Jupiter) is covered in an icy surface that may be 30 km thick. In comparison, the ice sheet on Antarctica is just 4.8 km thick.

ICE

CRUST

EUROPA
JUPITER

ICE

CRUST

ANTARCTICA
EARTH

VOLCANOES

24 KM

Volcanoes on the moon Io (Jupiter) throw plumes of material up to 300 km high above the surface. In comparison, the eruption of Mount St Helens in 1980 threw a cloud of ash up to altitudes of just 24 km.

MOON COUNT

JUPITER **MORE THAN 60**

SATURN **MORE THAN 60**

URANUS **27**

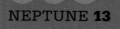

NEPTUNE **13**

MARS **2**   EARTH **1**

SMALL MOONS

Many moons in the Solar System are small and irregularly shaped. Earth's Moon is more than 200 times the width of Mars's tiny moons, Phobos and Deimos.

1610

The year the Italian scientist Galileo Galilei discovered the largest four moons around Jupiter: Callisto, Ganymede, Europa and Io.

DEIMOS
MARS

15 KM

MANHATTAN,
NEW YORK, USA

21.5 KM

Mars's moon **Phobos** has a declining orbit. This means that it will be **torn apart** by gravity in **10 million** years' time.

SMALL BODIES

As well as the planets, the Solar System contains millions of small bodies. These include dwarf planets, asteroids and comets.

THE ASTEROID BELT

Small pieces of rock that orbit the Sun are called asteroids, or, if they are quite large, they are called dwarf planets. Most of these lie in the Asteroid Belt between Mars and Jupiter.

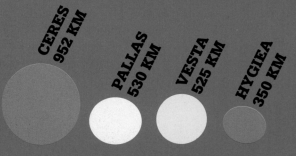

CERES 952 KM

PALLAS 530 KM

VESTA 525 KM

HYGIEA 350 KM

ABOUT HALF THE MASS OF THE BELT IS CONTAINED IN THE FOUR LARGEST ASTEROIDS

952 KM

The diameter of Ceres is 952 km, making it the biggest asteroid in the Asteroid Belt. Ceres is so big that it is called a dwarf planet.

ASTEROID BELT (NOT TO SCALE)

MARS

JUPITER

CERES

EARTH 12,756 KM

COMETS

Comets are lumps of ice, dust and grit that orbit the Sun. A comet's tail will only form as it approaches the Sun.

ORBIT OF COMET

SUN

TAIL

TAIL POINTS AWAY FROM SUN

VENUS

MERCURY

SUN

EARTH

According to **NASA**, there are about **1,290** asteroids that we know of that could **crash into** Earth.

COLLISION!

Sometimes, asteroids and comets slam into planets and moons. When this happens, they create enormous holes in the ground, called craters.

1. Asteroid or comet hits, throwing debris up and out.

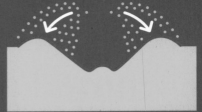

2. The debris settles around the hole creating the lip of the crater.

3. The centre of the hole rises, creating a bulge in the middle.

THE SUN

Our nearest star is the Sun. Far below its surface, tiny atoms are squeezed and squashed until they fuse together. This releases a huge amount of energy, which escapes as light and heat.

INSIDE THE SUN

The atomic reactions that create the Sun's heat and light happen deep inside its core. The energy released can take 100,000 years to travel through the upper layers before reaching the surface.

PHOTOSPHERE

CONVECTION ZONE

RADIATIVE ZONE

CORE

EARTH

,000,000

NUMBER OF TIMES THE EARTH COULD FIT INSIDE THE SUN

SUN

Temperature inside the core

15,000,000°C

SUNSPOTS

These are dark spots that appear on the Sun's surface.

5,500°C

SOLAR FLARE

This is a massive eruption of burning gas that leaps from the Sun's surface.

SOLAR PARTICLES

The Sun throws out a stream of particles called the solar wind. These particles are deflected towards the Earth's poles by the planet's magnetic field. Here, they react with the atmosphere to create the glowing lights of the aurorae.

NORTH POLE

SOUTH POLE

EARTH'S MAGNETIC FIELD

INCOMING SOLAR PARTICLES

TWINKLE, TWINKLE

Far beyond our Solar System lie trillions of other stars. These stars come in a range of sizes and colours and are often found grouped together in multiple systems or clusters.

MULTIPLES

While the Solar System has only one star, the Sun, many other stars are part of multiple star systems, which contain two or more stars. In fact, most of the stars we can see in the night sky belong to multiple systems.

COLOURS AND SIZES

A star's colour depends on its temperature. Stars that are white and blue are hotter than those that are yellow, orange or red. The largest stars are giants and supergiants, which can be more than 1,000 times bigger than the Sun.

SUN · SIRIUS · POLLUX · ARCTURUS

RIGEL

STAR LIFE AND DEATH

They may look like they shine for ever, but stars are born, live and then die. Depending on how massive they are, they can end their lives as a tiny white dwarf that gradually fades away, or as a powerful black hole, swallowing everything near it.

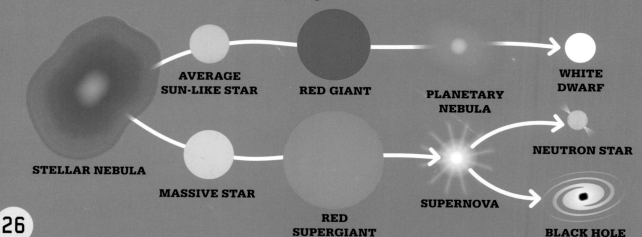

STELLAR NEBULA

AVERAGE SUN-LIKE STAR

RED GIANT

PLANETARY NEBULA

WHITE DWARF

MASSIVE STAR

RED SUPERGIANT

SUPERNOVA

NEUTRON STAR

BLACK HOLE

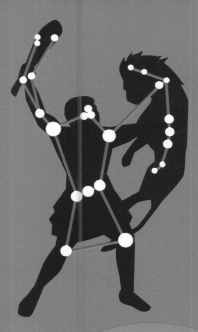

CONSTELLATIONS

We group the stars we can see in the night sky into pictures and patterns called constellations. Many of these are named after mythical figures, such as Orion the hunter.

88

THE NUMBER OF CONSTELLATIONS INTO WHICH THE NIGHT SKY IS DIVIDED.

ALDEBARAN

BETELGEUSE

SIZE OF THE SWOLLEN SUN

BLACK HOLES

A black hole is an object that is left behind after a massive star dies. Scientists are unsure what black holes are exactly, but they have so much gravity that not even light can escape from them.

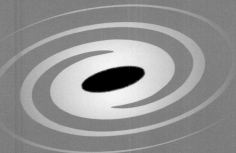

SUN ·······>

AT THE END OF ITS LIFE, THE SUN WILL SWELL UP TO FORM A RED GIANT STAR. THIS WILL HAPPEN IN

7,000,000,000 YEARS.

THE MILKY WAY

Stars are grouped together in enormous structures called galaxies. Our galaxy is called the Milky Way and it contains about 200 billion stars.

OUR GALAXY

If you could look down on the Milky Way, it would have a spiral shape, with the stars collected into several arms that orbit around a large centre, called the galactic core. The Milky Way is 100,000 light years across.

10,000 LY

20,000 LY

30,000 LY

40,000 LY

50,000 LY

CARINA-SAGITTARIUS ARM

LIGHT YEARS

Distances in space are so big that astronomers cannot use normal units, such as kilometres. Instead, they use the distance that light can travel in a year. This is called a light year (LY).

PERSEUS ARM

ORION SPUR

OUTER ARM

SUN

SPIRAL ARMS
The Sun and its nearest stars
form part of a small arm of
the Milky Way called the
Orion Spur.

LONG BAR

GALACTIC BAR

CRUX-SCUTUM
ARM

GALAXY CENTRE
This measures about 10,000
light years across and is about
6,000 light years thick.

DISTANCE LIGHT WILL TRAVEL IN A
NANOSECOND (ONE BILLIONTH OF A SECOND) → **30 CM**

GALAXIES

The Milky Way is just one of many galaxies that make up the Universe. These enormous objects come in many shapes and sizes and are grouped together in clusters and superclusters.

GALAXY SIZES

While the Milky Way contains some 200 billion stars, our nearest major galaxy, the Andromeda Galaxy, contains up to 400 billion, and is about 200,000 light years in diameter.

200 BILLION

400 BILLION

GALAXY TYPES

ELLIPTICAL
These galaxies range from ball-shaped to oval. They usually have very old stars in them and tend to be much larger than other types of galaxy.

LENTICULAR
Like spiral galaxies, lenticular galaxies have a large central bulge surrounded by a disc. But this disc does not have the curving arms of spiral galaxies.

IRREGULAR
As their name suggests, these galaxies have no clear shape at all.

6,000,000, LY

GALAXY NUMBERS

There are about 170 billion galaxies in the observable Universe (the part of the Universe we can see).

170,000,000,000

BARRED SPIRAL

This is a type of spiral galaxy that has a long bar running through the centre. The size of this bar can vary greatly.

SPIRAL

Spiral galaxies have a large central core that is surrounded by a disc. Stars spiral out along this disc in huge curving arms.

60%

OF ALL KNOWN GALAXIES ARE SPIRAL-SHAPED

COLLIDING

Sometimes, galaxies slam into each other. They will either tear each other apart, or crash together and combine to form a new, larger galaxy.

THE BIGGEST GALAXIES FOUND MEASURE 6 MILLION LIGHT YEARS ACROSS – THE MILKY WAY IS ONLY ABOUT 100,000 LY.

Many galaxies are found collected together in small groups, which contain up to 50 galaxies, or in clusters, which contain between 50 and several thousand galaxies.

IN TURN, THESE ARE CLUMPED TOGETHER TO FORM SUPERCLUSTERS.

THE SUPERCLUSTER WHICH CONTAINS THE MILKY WAY MEASURES

110 MILLION

LIGHT YEARS ACROSS AND IS MADE UP OF 50,000 GALAXIES.

The Milky Way and Andromeda

galaxies are heading towards

each other at

300 km per second and will

collide and merge in about

5,000,000,000

years' time.

THE BIG BANG

Scientists can see that all of the distant galaxies are moving away from each other. This indicates that at some time, long ago, everything was much closer together than it is today.

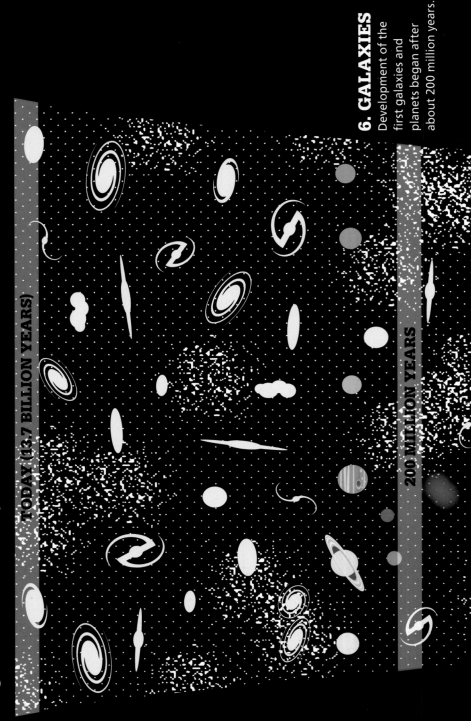

TODAY (13.7 BILLION YEARS)

200 MILLION YEARS

6. GALAXIES

Development of the first galaxies and planets began after about 200 million years.

5. SHINING STARS

The first stars started to shine about 100 million years after the Big Bang.

3. COOLING OFF

After expanding rapidly, space cooled, allowing tiny subatomic particles (electrons, neutrons and protons) to form.

100 MILLION YEARS

500,000 YEARS

3 MINUTES

1 SECOND

1. THE BIG BANG

Scientists believe that the Universe was created in an enormous explosion, which formed all matter. This is also referred to as the Big Bang.

4. ATOMS FORM

Electrons, neutrons and protons combined to form the first atoms about 300,000 years after the Big Bang.

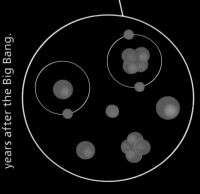

2. INFLATION

In the first few minutes after the Big Bang, the Universe expanded very quickly. During this time, it was like a boiling soup, made up of super-hot particles.

STUDYING SPACE

Astronomers use different telescopes to collect information about the night sky. These telescopes detect the light we can see as well as the energy we cannot, such as infra-red and microwaves, to build up a complete picture of the Universe.

1608 THE YEAR THE FIRST WORKING TELESCOPES WERE MADE.

27
The Very Large Array in New Mexico, USA, is a collection of 27 individual radio dishes that can operate together.

30 M
THE SIZE OF THE MIRROR ON THE NEW TELESCOPE AT MAUNA KEA, HAWAII. IT IS DUE TO BE COMPLETED IN 2018.

305 M
The radio telescope of the Arecibo Observatory in Puerto Rico measures 305 metres across. The enormous dish is set into a natural hollow in a mountain.

RADIO TELESCOPES ARE DISH-SHAPED ANTENNAS. THEY COLLECT THE INVISIBLE RADIO WAVES THAT ARE PRODUCED BY MOST BODIES IN SPACE.

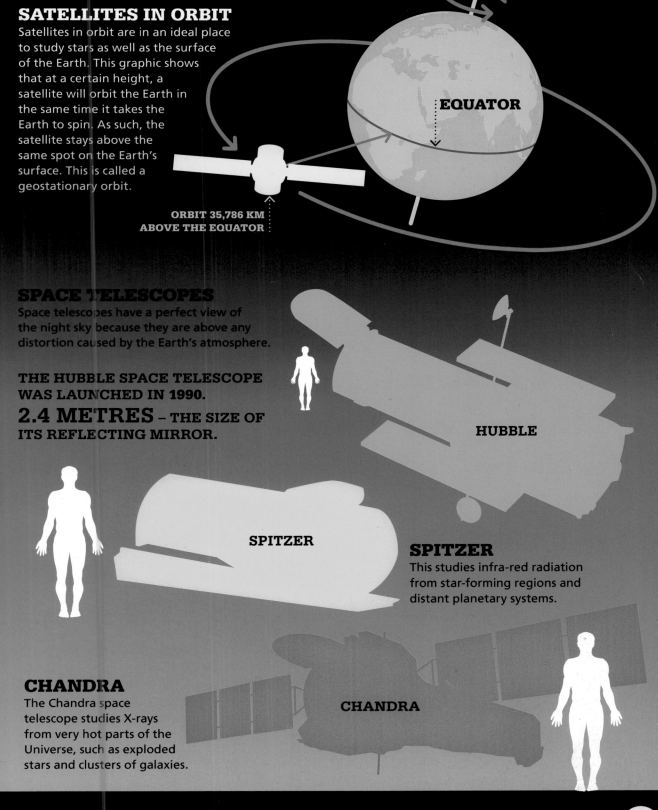

SATELLITES IN ORBIT

Satellites in orbit are in an ideal place to study stars as well as the surface of the Earth. This graphic shows that at a certain height, a satellite will orbit the Earth in the same time it takes the Earth to spin. As such, the satellite stays above the same spot on the Earth's surface. This is called a geostationary orbit.

EQUATOR

ORBIT 35,786 KM ABOVE THE EQUATOR

SPACE TELESCOPES

Space telescopes have a perfect view of the night sky because they are above any distortion caused by the Earth's atmosphere.

THE HUBBLE SPACE TELESCOPE WAS LAUNCHED IN 1990.
2.4 METRES – THE SIZE OF ITS REFLECTING MIRROR.

HUBBLE

SPITZER

SPITZER

This studies infra-red radiation from star-forming regions and distant planetary systems.

CHANDRA

The Chandra space telescope studies X-rays from very hot parts of the Universe, such as exploded stars and clusters of galaxies.

CHANDRA

RADIO TELESCOPES CAN USE A SINGLE ANTENNA, OR SEVERAL ANTENNAS CAN BE JOINED TOGETHER TO MAKE A BETTER IMAGE.

EXPLORING SPACE

Spacecraft have been blasted to every planet in the Solar System, sending back pictures and rock samples. Humans have even left the Earth and walked on the Moon.

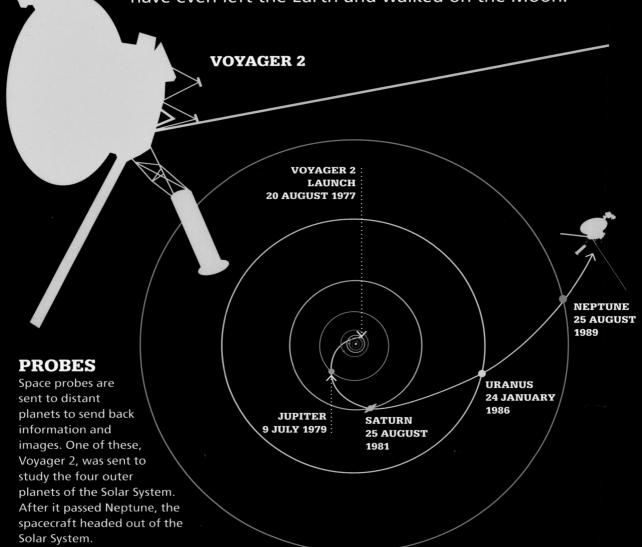

VOYAGER 2

VOYAGER 2
LAUNCH
20 AUGUST 1977

NEPTUNE
25 AUGUST
1989

URANUS
24 JANUARY
1986

JUPITER
9 JULY 1979

SATURN
25 AUGUST
1981

PROBES

Space probes are sent to distant planets to send back information and images. One of these, Voyager 2, was sent to study the four outer planets of the Solar System. After it passed Neptune, the spacecraft headed out of the Solar System.

Distance of Voyager 2 from Earth at the start of 2012

14,600,000,000 KM

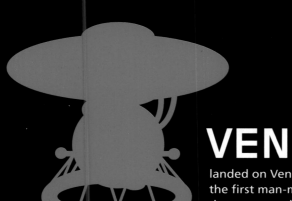

1957
Year the first object, Sputnik 1, was sent into space.

VENERA 7
landed on Venus in 1970 and became the first man-made spacecraft to touch down on another planet and to transmit data back to Earth.

MAN ON THE MOON
Twelve astronauts landed on the Moon during six Apollo missions. The last person to walk on the Moon was Eugene Cernan during the Apollo 17 mission in 1972.

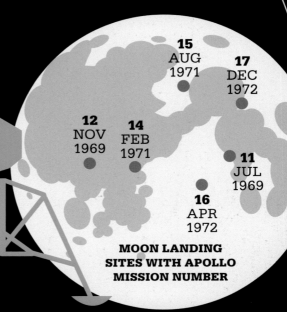

15 AUG 1971

17 DEC 1972

12 NOV 1969

14 FEB 1971

11 JUL 1969

16 APR 1972

MOON LANDING SITES WITH APOLLO MISSION NUMBER

INTERNATIONAL SPACE STATION

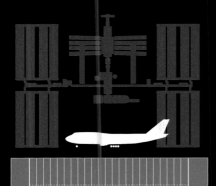

A space station is a spacecraft that can carry a crew and stay in orbit around Earth for a long period of time.

THE INTERNATIONAL SPACE STATION IS ABOUT THE SAME SIZE AS AN AMERICAN FOOTBALL FIELD.

IN ITS FIRST 10 YEARS, IT TRAVELLED ALMOST

2,500,000,000
KILOMETRES IN 57,361 ORBITS AROUND EARTH.

That is the same as eight trips to the Sun and back.

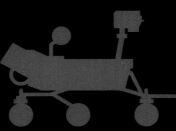

CURIOSITY
Rovers are a type of robot spacecraft that move around a planet's surface. Curiosity is the size of a small car and was designed to explore the surface of Mars, looking for signs of life.

INSIDE THE EARTH

Slicing the entire Earth in half would show that its inside is divided into different layers. These layers push down on each other, creating high pressures and temperatures inside the planet.

CRUST

INNER AND OUTER CORE

MANTLE

0.4%

The crust makes up just 0.4 per cent of the Earth's mass, the core makes up about 30 per cent, while the mantle makes up nearly 70 per cent.

MANTLE 100 KM TO 2,900 KM

OUTER CORE 2,900 KM TO 5,100 KM

6,378 km

The distance from the surface to the centre of the Earth (6,378 km) is the same as flying from London to Chicago.

The temperature inside the Earth increases with **depth**. This is called the **geothermal gradient**.

41

WARMING UP

The pressures and temperatures inside the Earth are high enough to melt rock.

CRUST UP TO A DEPTH OF 100 KM

INNER CORE 5,100 KM TO 6,378 KM

MOLTEN ROCK IS CONSTANTLY ON THE MOVE

4,900–6,100°C

INNER CORE 4,900-6,100°C

OUTER CORE 4,500-5,000°C

SURFACE **AVERAGE 15°C**

The inner core is **as hot as** the surface of the **Sun**.

ON THE MOVE

The Earth's crust is broken up into tectonic plates. As the molten rock of the mantle swirls about under the crust, it pushes and pulls these plates around.

TRANSFORM BOUNDARY

where two plates rub against each other

DIVERGENT BOUNDARY

where two plates pull apart from each other

ARCTIC RIDGE

NORTH AMERICAN PLATE

JUAN DE FUCA PLATE

CARIBBEAN PLATE

AFRICAN PLATE

PACIFIC PLATE

COCOS PLATE

EAST PACIFIC RISE

NAZCA PLATE

SOUTH AMERICAN PLATE

SCOTIA PLATE

ANTARCTIC PLATE

Plate boundaries

The place where two plates meet is called a boundary. Plates rub together, pull apart or slam into each other. This movement of the crust between two plates can cause volcanic activity and earthquakes.

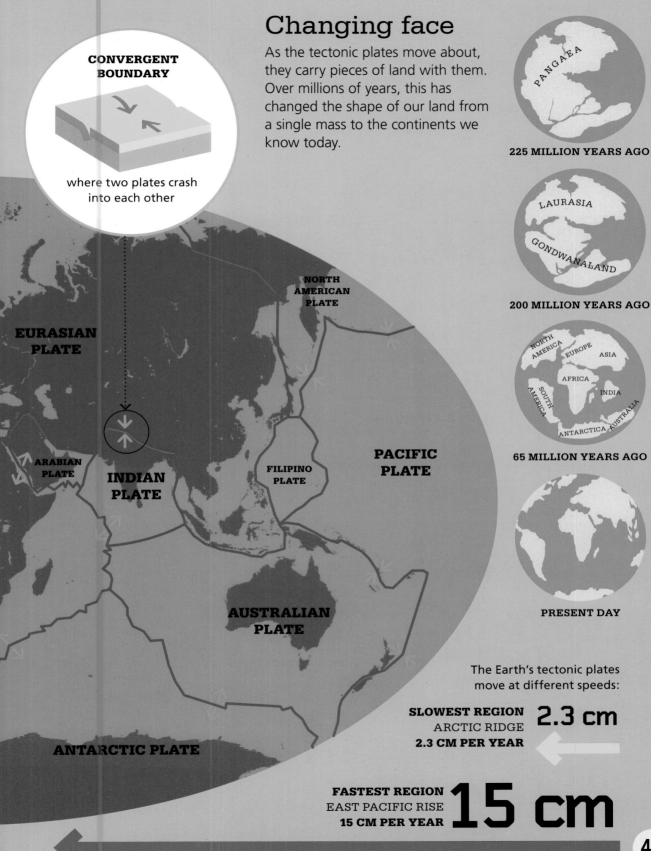

CONVERGENT BOUNDARY

where two plates crash into each other

Changing face

As the tectonic plates move about, they carry pieces of land with them. Over millions of years, this has changed the shape of our land from a single mass to the continents we know today.

PANGAEA

225 MILLION YEARS AGO

LAURASIA

GONDWANALAND

200 MILLION YEARS AGO

NORTH AMERICA

EUROPE

ASIA

AFRICA

SOUTH AMERICA

INDIA

AUSTRALIA

ANTARCTICA

65 MILLION YEARS AGO

PRESENT DAY

EURASIAN PLATE

NORTH AMERICAN PLATE

ARABIAN PLATE

INDIAN PLATE

FILIPINO PLATE

PACIFIC PLATE

AUSTRALIAN PLATE

ANTARCTIC PLATE

The Earth's tectonic plates move at different speeds:

SLOWEST REGION
ARCTIC RIDGE
2.3 CM PER YEAR

2.3 cm

FASTEST REGION
EAST PACIFIC RISE
15 CM PER YEAR

15 cm

RESTLESS EARTH

The Earth's moving tectonic plates sometimes catch against each other and get stuck, before releasing suddenly. This sudden release causes earthquakes.

Strong or weak?

The strength of an earthquake is known as its magnitude. This is measured by the Richter scale – the higher the number, the stronger the earthquake. The scale has no upper limit, but no earthquake with a magnitude of 10 or higher has ever been recorded.

830,000

Death toll in the deadliest earthquake ever recorded. It occurred in the Shaanxi province of China in 1556.

7.8
1906 SAN FRANCISCO (USA)

8.0
1985 MEXICO CITY (MEXICO)

8.1
1650 CUZCO (PERU)

9.5
1960 VALDIVIA AND PUERTO MONTT (CHILE)

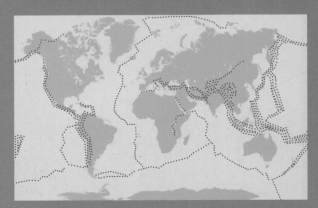

This map (left) highlights where major earthquakes occur. Most earthquakes occur at or near plate boundaries.

8.5

THE MOST POWERFUL NUCLEAR EXPLOSION, THE TSAR BOMBA, WAS DETONATED IN 1961. IT RELEASED THE SAME AMOUNT OF ENERGY AS AN EARTHQUAKE MEASURING 8.5 ON THE RICHTER SCALE.

MOST

Many countries can claim to have the most earthquakes, including Japan, Indonesia, Fiji, Tonga, China and Iran.

7.7
1780 TABRIZ (IRAN)

9.0
2011 HONSHU (JAPAN)

9.1
2004 ACEH PROVINCE (INDONESIA)

Of **500,000** earthquakes that are detected each year (several million actually occur each year), **100,000** can be felt and **100** cause any damage.

MAGNITUDE	NUMBER
2–2.9	1,300,000
3–3.9	130,000
4–4.9	13,000
5–5.9	1,319
6–6.9	134
7–7.9	15
8.0+	1

NUMBER AND MAGNITUDE OF EARTHQUAKES PER YEAR

FEWEST

Small earthquakes can occur anywhere, but Antarctica is the continent with the fewest earthquakes.

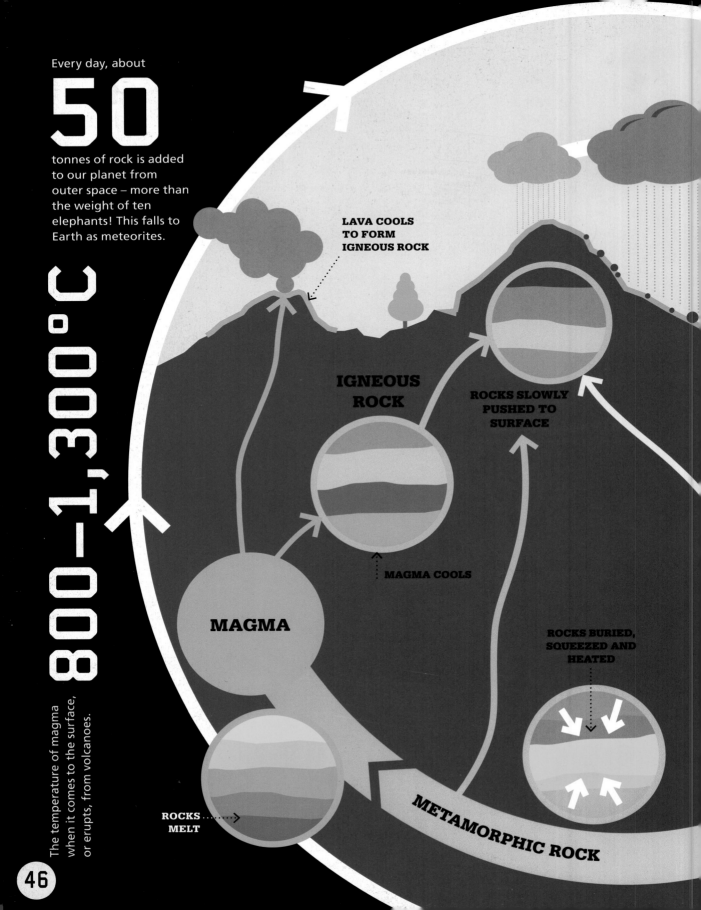

Every day, about

50

tonnes of rock is added to our planet from outer space – more than the weight of ten elephants! This falls to Earth as meteorites.

800–1,300°C

The temperature of magma when it comes to the surface, or erupts, from volcanoes.

LAVA COOLS
TO FORM
IGNEOUS ROCK

IGNEOUS
ROCK

ROCKS SLOWLY
PUSHED TO
SURFACE

MAGMA COOLS

MAGMA

ROCKS BURIED,
SQUEEZED AND
HEATED

ROCKS MELT

METAMORPHIC ROCK

THE ROCK CYCLE

As the Earth's tectonic plates move about, rock is pushed down into the Earth, where it melts. Other rock is pushed up to the surface, where it is worn away or eroded by wind, ice and water. These changes in rocks are part of the rock cycle.

RAIN AND WIND ERODE ROCKS

ROCK PARTICLES TRANSPORTED BY RIVERS

ROCK PARTICLES FALL TO SEA FLOOR

LAYERS OF ROCK SQUEEZED TOGETHER

SEDIMENTARY ROCK

Rock types

There are three types of rock. Igneous rocks are formed from molten rock. Sedimentary rock is formed when tiny pieces of rock settle at the bottom of the sea where they are compressed. Metamorphic rock is formed when rocks are changed through heat and pressure.

80%

About 80 per cent of the rocks at the Earth's surface are sedimentary.

VIOLENT VOLCANOES

Volcanoes form when molten rock travels up from the Earth's mantle and erupts onto the surface. These eruptions can be quick and explosive or long and relatively peaceful.

TYPES OF VOLCANO

After lava erupts out of a volcano, it cools to form solid rock, creating the cone of the volcano. The shape of the cone depends on the type of lava. For example, runny lava creates a low, wide shield volcano.

SHIELD VOLCANO

COMPOUND/COMPLEX VOLCANO WITH AN OLD CONE

STRATOVOLCANO

CALDERA VOLCANO

YELLOWSTONE
HUCKLEBERRY RIDGE

(2.1 MYA)
2,450 KM³

ENOUGH TO FILL GREAT BEAR LAKE, CANADA

BIGGEST ERUPTIONS

This infographic shows the amount of magma produced by some of the biggest eruptions, along with their dates (MYA is 'millions of years ago'). The eruption at Toba was the largest ever.

ASH CLOUD

In 1991, the eruption of Mount Pinatubo sent an enormous cloud of ash to heights of 34 kilometres. The cloud covered an area of 125,000 sq km – that is about half the size of the UK.

THE EXPLOSION OF KRAKATOA IN 1883 HAD A FORCE EQUIVALENT TO

10,000

ATOMIC BOMBS

FORMING A CORAL ATOLL

1. Volcanic cone forms above sea level.

2. When volcano stops erupting, a ring of coral, called an atoll, forms around the cone.

3. Coral continues to grow, while the volcano cone is eroded.

4. Volcano cone eroded below sea level, leaving atoll above water.

YELLOWSTONE MESA FALLS (1.3 MYA)
280 KM³

LONG VALLEY CALDERA (760,000 YA)
600 KM³

YELLOWSTONE LAVA CREEK (640,000 YA)
1,000 KM³

TOBA
(74,000 YA)
2,800 KM³
ENOUGH TO FILL LAKE VICTORIA, AFRICA

TOWERING PEAKS

Where tectonic plates crash into each other, they can push the ground up to form mountains. Mountains are often grouped together in long chains near plate boundaries.

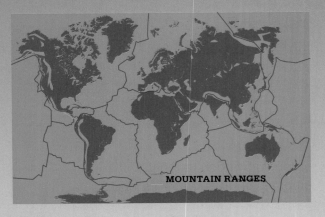

MOUNTAIN RANGES

The tallest mountain in the world is part of the Himalayas mountain range.

This is the tallest peak in the Andes, which run the length of South America.

EVEREST
ASIA
8,848 m

ACONCAGUA
SOUTH AMERICA
6,962 m

ELBRUS
EUROPE
5,642 m

The tallest peak in Europe is a volcano that is part of the Caucasus range, which lies in Russia near the border with Georgia.

Changes

Conditions and climate change as you climb up a mountain, affecting the kinds of plants and animals that can live at different heights. Places that are higher up a mountain will be colder and may well be wetter that those lower down. Anything living here will have to adapt to these conditions.

ALPINE ZONE

SNOW LINE

TREE LINE

SUBALPINE ZONE
UP TO 3,970 m

TEMPERATE ZONE
UP TO 2,440 m

SUBTROPICAL ZONE
UP TO 1,830 m

16,000 km

The world's longest mountain range is the Mid-Atlantic Ridge. It runs along the entire length of the Atlantic Ocean and is completely submerged.

The tallest peak in North America was formed by a collision between the Pacific and North American plates.

Kilimanjaro is the highest peak in Africa and is not part of a mountain chain.

MT McKINLEY (DENALI)
NORTH AMERICA
6,194 m

KILIMANJARO
AFRICA
5,895 m

VINSON MASSIF
ANTARCTICA
4,897 m

Part of the Ellsworth Mountains, this peak is just 1,200 km from the South Pole.

CARSTENSZ PYRAMID
OCEANIA
4,884 m

Located on New Guinea, this mountain was formed by a collision between the Australian and Pacific plates.

51

HABITATS

From teeming coral reefs to densely packed forests, the world is covered in a wide range of different habitats. The type of habitat is decided by what the climatic conditions are in a region.

POLAR AND TUNDRA

TEMPERATE FOREST

SAVANNAH

TROPICAL FOREST

MOUNTAIN VEGETATION

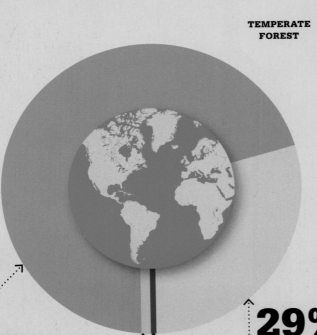

71%
OF EARTH IS AQUATIC OF WHICH...

29%
OF EARTH IS LAND

1% IS COVERED BY CORAL REEFS

2.5% IS FRESHWATER

29%
OF EARTH IS LAND OF WHICH...

31% DESERT
INCLUDING THE POLES

33% GRASSLAND
INCLUDING TEMPERATE GRASSLAND AND SAVANNAH

36% FOREST
INCLUDING TROPICAL AND CONIFEROUS FOREST (TAIGA)

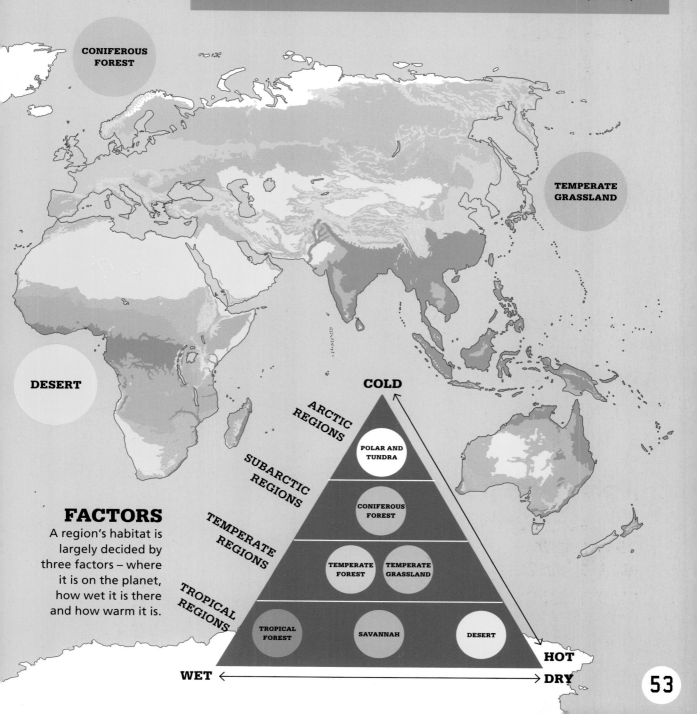

CONIFEROUS FOREST

TEMPERATE GRASSLAND

DESERT

FACTORS

A region's habitat is largely decided by three factors – where it is on the planet, how wet it is there and how warm it is.

COLD

ARCTIC REGIONS

SUBARCTIC REGIONS

TEMPERATE REGIONS

TROPICAL REGIONS

POLAR AND TUNDRA

CONIFEROUS FOREST

TEMPERATE FOREST

TEMPERATE GRASSLAND

TROPICAL FOREST

SAVANNAH

DESERT

HOT

WET ← → DRY

THE AIR WE BREATHE

Surrounding our planet is a thin layer of gases called the atmosphere. It contains the air that is vital for us to live and it produces all of our weather.

THERMOSPHERE
85–640 KM

SPACESHIPONE
FIRST MANNED PRIVATE
SPACEFLIGHT 112 KM

MESOSPHERE
50–85 KM

STRATO-LAB V
HIGHEST MANNED BALLOON 34 KM ···→

STRATOSPHERE
18–50 KM

MODERN PASSENGER JET
CRUISING ALTITUDE 10 KM

CIRRUS

CIRROSTRATUS

ALTOCUMULUS

NIMBOSTRATUS

CUMULONIMBUS

STRATUS **CUMULUS**
TROPOSPHERE
WITH CLOUDS
UP TO 18 KM

WIND SPEED

As air is heated by the Sun, it starts to move around, creating wind. Wind speed is measured using the Beaufort scale. A measure of one is almost still, while 12 will blow down buildings.

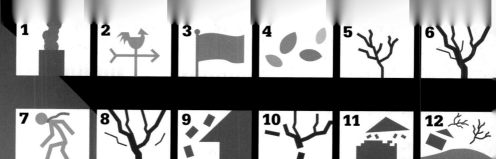

1 2 3 4 5 6

7 8 9 10 11 12

HUBBLE SPACE TELESCOPE
559 KM

EXOSPHERE
ABOVE 640 KM

ISS
278–460 KM

408 km/h

The fastest wind speed ever recorded. It was measured at an automatic weather station on Barrow Island, Australia, during tropical cyclone Olivia on 10 April 1996.

78.08%
NITROGEN

20.95%
OXYGEN

0–4%
WATER VAPOUR

0.93%
ARGON

0.038%
CARBON DIOXIDE

What's in air?

Most of the air we breathe in is made up of the gas nitrogen. About one-fifth of air is made up of oxygen, which is the gas we need to stay alive. There are also tiny amounts of other gases, including argon and carbon dioxide.

WATER CYCLE

Water is vital for life. It also plays an important part in the weather and in shaping the land. Water moves around our planet in a system called the water cycle.

1,000,000,000,000,000

EACH DAY, THE SUN CAUSES ONE TRILLION TONNES OF WATER TO EVAPORATE.

CONDENSATION

80%
OF THE EARTH'S WATER IS SURFACE WATER.

20% IS EITHER GROUNDWATER OR ATMOSPHERIC WATER VAPOUR.

TRANSPIRATION
FROM PLANTS

EVAPORATION
FROM OCEANS AND LAKES

505,000 KM³

The volume of water that falls as precipitation each year all around the Earth.

PRECIPITATION

SNOW MELT

434,000 KM³

The amount of water that evaporates from the Earth's oceans in a year.

Nearly **all** of the water found in the atmosphere lies within the **troposphere**, the part of the atmosphere below **18 km**.

SURFACE RUNOFF

GROUNDWATER

OCEANS AND LAKES

3%

The average amount of salt and minerals found in seawater.

WATER WORLD

Water covers 71 per cent of the Earth's surface, in seas, oceans and rivers. But water is also found in the air we breathe and frozen in the ice caps near the poles. Just how much water is there on our planet?

1.4 BILLION KM³

The total volume of all the water on our planet and in the atmosphere.

EARTH'S DIAMETER 12,756 KM

IF THE WORLD'S WATER WERE MADE INTO A BALL, IT WOULD MEASURE 1,390 KM ACROSS. ·············>

ICEBERG B15 295 KM LONG

The world's largest iceberg, called B15, broke away from Antarctica in 2000. Parts of it still haven't melted.

JAMAICA 234 KM LONG

MASS OF ICEBERG B15 WAS THREE BILLION TONNES **3,000,000,000**

FRESH WATER **2.5%**
OF THIS…

SALTWATER IN
OCEANS, SEAS,
GROUNDWATER
AND LAKES

97.5%

GLACIERS
68.7%

GROUNDWATER
30.1%

PERMANENTLY FROZEN IN THE
GROUND (PERMAFROST) **0.8%**

WATER IN THE AIR AND ON THE
EARTH'S SURFACE **0.4%**

Most in one minute: 31.2 mm; Unionville, Maryland, USA, 4 July 1956

Most in 60 minutes: 305 mm in 42 minutes; Holt, Missouri, USA, 22 June 1947

Most in 24 hours: 1,825 mm; Foc-Foc, Réunion, 7–8 January 1966

Most in 12 hours: 1,144 mm; Foc-Foc, Réunion, 8 January 1966, during tropical cyclone Denise

Most in 48 hours: 2,467 mm; Aurère, Réunion, 8–10 January 1958

Most in 72 hours: 3,929 mm; Commerson, Réunion, 24–26 February 2007

Most in 96 hours: 4,869 mm; Commerson, Réunion, 24–27 February 2007

Most in one year: 26,470 mm; Cherrapunji, India, 1860–1861

Highest average annual total: 11,872 mm; Mawsynram, India

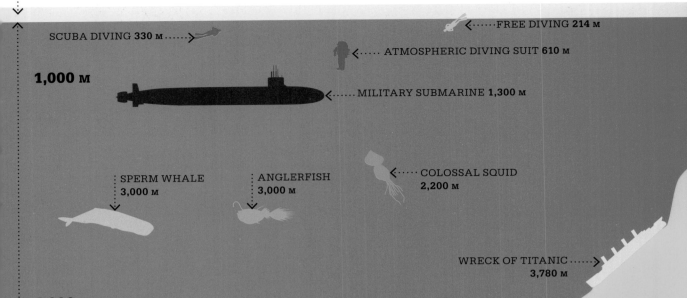

SCUBA DIVING 330 M ......>

FREE DIVING 214 M

ATMOSPHERIC DIVING SUIT 610 M

1,000 M

MILITARY SUBMARINE 1,300 M

SPERM WHALE 3,000 M

ANGLERFISH 3,000 M

COLOSSAL SQUID 2,200 M

WRECK OF TITANIC ......> 3,780 M

4,000 M

APHOTIC

THE OCEANS

Beneath the surface of the Earth's seas and oceans is a varied world of different regions that reach down to the darkest depths.

CUSK-EEL 8,370 M

8,000 M

Under pressure

The oceans are divided into different zones. The photic zone is part of the ocean where sunlight can reach. Beneath it is the dark aphotic zone. Pressures become greater as depths increase. Just 10 m below the waves, the pressure is already twice that at the surface.

THE SUBMERSIBLE *TRIESTE* HOLDS THE RECORD FOR THE DEEPEST DIVE EVER MADE – 10,911 M BELOW THE SURFACE.

10,911 M

TRIESTE

46.5%

The percentage of the world's oceans made up by the Pacific – almost as much as the Indian, Atlantic, Southern and Arctic Oceans put together.

6% .... SOUTHERN OCEAN

4.1% ARCTIC OCEAN

20.5% INDIAN OCEAN

22.9% ATLANTIC OCEAN

46.5% PACIFIC OCEAN

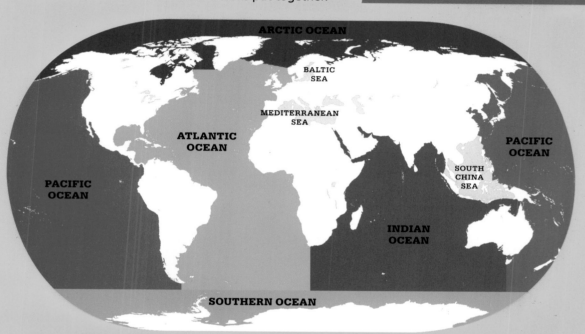

ARCTIC OCEAN

BALTIC SEA

MEDITERRANEAN SEA

ATLANTIC OCEAN

PACIFIC OCEAN

SOUTH CHINA SEA

PACIFIC OCEAN

INDIAN OCEAN

SOUTHERN OCEAN

If all the **salt** were taken out of the ocean it would cover all the land to a depth of

1.5 metres

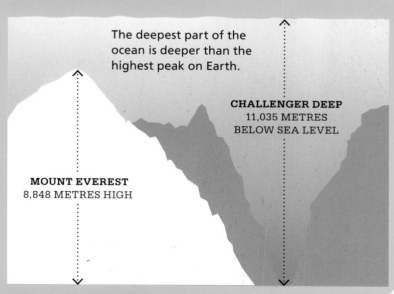

The deepest part of the ocean is deeper than the highest peak on Earth.

CHALLENGER DEEP
11,035 METRES
BELOW SEA LEVEL

MOUNT EVEREST
8,848 METRES HIGH

RAGING RIVERS

Some of the Earth's rivers are so big that they stretch for thousands of kilometres. They tumble over towering waterfalls and meander through the countryside, carrying enormous amounts of water across the land.

	source	countries crossed
NILE	LAKE VICTORIA	ETHIOPIA SUDAN SOUTH SUDAN EGYPT UGANDA TANZANIA RWANDA DEMOCRATIC REPUBLIC OF THE CONGO KENYA BURUNDI ERITREA
AMAZON-UCYALI-APURIMAC	ANDES MOUNTAINS	BRAZIL COLOMBIA ECUADOR PERU
YANGTZE	TANGGULA MOUNTAINS	CHINA
MISSISSIPPI-MISSOURI-RED ROCK	LAKE ITASCA	UNITED STATES
YENISEY-BAIKAL-SELENGA	MUNGARAGIYN-GOL	MONGOLIA RUSSIA
HUANG HE (YELLOW)	BAYAN HAR MOUNTAINS	CHINA
OB-IRTYSH	BELUKHA MOUNTAIN	RUSSIA
PARANÁ	RIO PARANAÍBA	ARGENTINA BRAZIL PARAGUAY
	source	countries crossed

River discharge

The amount of water that a river releases into a sea or lake is called its discharge. A river's discharge depends on the local climate and the size of its drainage basin, which is the area of land that the river empties of water.

The world's **20** largest rivers **discharge** enough water to fill a **football stadium** in **3** seconds.

RIVERS WITH THE GREATEST DISCHARGE

RIO NEGRO
28,400 m³/s

MADEIRA
31,200 m³/s

ORINOCO
33,000 m³/s

YANGTZE
35,000 m³/s

250,000

The number of rivers there are in the USA, with a combined total length of more than 5.6 million kilometres.

If you put the 20 longest rivers end to end they would wrap around the equator more than

twice

ends	length
MEDITERRANEAN SEA	6,650 km
ATLANTIC OCEAN	6,400 km
EAST CHINA SEA	6,300 km
GULF OF MEXICO	5,971 km
YENISEI GULF	5,540 km
BOHAI SEA	5,465 km
GULF OF OB	5,410 km
RIO DE LA PLATA	4,880 km

ends — length

CONGO
41,200 m³/s

GANGES
42,470 m³/s

AMAZON
175,000 m³/s

Angel Falls, Venezuela **979 m**

3 Eiffel Towers

HIGHEST WATERFALL IN THE WORLD

CHANGING EARTH

Conditions on our planet are not fixed. During the Earth's history there have been long periods of the planet heating up and then cooling down. Scientists have discovered that, at present, the Earth is getting warmer.

REFLECTED
Some of the Sun's radiation is reflected back out into space by the Earth's surface.

LOST HEAT
When the Earth absorbs the Sun's radiation, it then produces its own radiation as infrared heat. Some of this heat is lost into space.

Rising seas

Increasing temperatures around the world could melt the ice caps at the poles. As a result, sea levels would rise. The red areas on the graphic above are those that would be flooded by a rise in sea levels of 10 m.

AEROSOLS

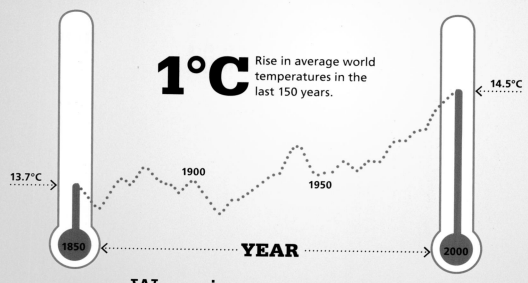

1°C Rise in average world temperatures in the last 150 years.

14.5°C

13.7°C

1900

1950

1850

YEAR

2000

Warming

Our planet is kept warm by a process called the greenhouse effect. Gases and other substances, such as aerosols, in the atmosphere trap the heat that is reflected or given off by the Earth.

SUN'S RAYS

Nearly three-quarters of the Sun's radiation that reaches the Earth makes it to the surface.

AEROSOLS

LOST IN SPACE

Some of the Sun's radiation is reflected straight back out into space.

GREENHOUSE

Gases and other substances in the atmosphere trap heat given off by the Earth, warming the atmosphere up even more and creating the greenhouse effect.

INCREASING DEMAND

Natural resources are naturally occuring substances that people can use to make objects, produce power or consume as food and drink. Many of these resources are limited, however, and their use is threatened by increasing demand.

A GROWING WORLD

At present, the world's population stands at more than 7 billion people. Over the next 60 years, improvements in health care and diet will see people living for longer and the world's population soar to more than 9 billion. This is more than twice the size it was 100 years before.

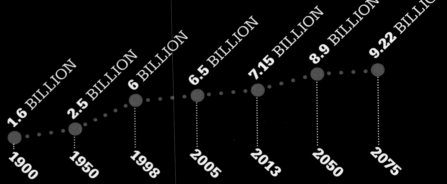

1.6 BILLION 1900
2.5 BILLION 1950
6 BILLION 1998
6.5 BILLION 2005
7.15 BILLION 2013
8.9 BILLION 2050
9.22 BILLION 2075

Projected world population figures

2013
150,000

2015
190,000

2020
280,000

(tonnes per year)

INCREASING DEMAND

Lithium is used to make batteries for hi-tech products, such as digital cameras. Increased demand for these will raise the need for this resource.

TANTALUM

Demand for this rare element that does not **corrode** has increased by 8–12 per cent each year since 1995, and **1,700 tonnes** is now produced each year.

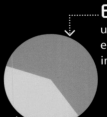

60% is used in the electronics industry

40% is used elsewhere, such as medicine and aircraft manufacture

Nearly 1.3 billion people do not have electricity. It would cost

US$1 TRILLION

to meet full demand by 2030.

MORE POWER

Increases in demand are not only due to an increase in the number of people. Better **living conditions** and improvements in supply will also increase demand. Up to 2035, rapid **industrialisation** in China and improvements in living conditions will see an increase in demand for electricity. Experts predict that demand for natural gas to fuel this increase will rise by more than

400%.

China's natural gas demand

2011
130
BILLION CUBIC METRES

2035
545
BILLION CUBIC METRES

How electricity is produced today

Oil and other liquids **1%**

Renewables **13%**

Nuclear **19%**

Natural gas **25%**

Coal **42%**

Electricity generation in the USA

69

THE OCEAN'S RESOURCES

Seas and oceans cover more than two-thirds of the planet's surface. These waters provide millions of tonnes of food. Other sources include rivers, vast inland seas and enormous fish farms where sea creatures are reared.

FISHING NETS

Large commercial fishing boats use huge nets to catch fish. Many people believe that these large nets catch too many fish, destroying fish numbers and even damaging the sea floor. They also trap other sea creatures, including dolphins and turtles.

midwater trawl

purse seine

tangle net

bottom trawl

Lobster catching is a multi-billion-dollar industry, with nearly

200,000 tonnes caught each year.

That is the mass of more than

550 JUMBO JETS

OTHER OCEAN RESOURCES

The world's ocean waters hold nearly **20 million tonnes** of gold – each litre of seawater has, on average, 13 billionths of a gram dissolved in it.

That is enough for

2.83 kg

for every person on the planet.

HOW MUCH IS CAUGHT?

Every year,
131 million tonnes of fish are caught and used for food – that is

18.8 kg
per person

the equivalent to **165 quarter-pounder burgers** for each person.

Where is it caught?

THE OCEANS' RICHEST FISHING GROUNDS

NW Pacific
20.9 million tonnes
(27%)

NE Atlantic
8.7 million tonnes
(11%)

West Central Pacific
11.7 million tonnes
(15%)

SE Pacific
7.8 million tonnes
(10%)

about
80
million tonnes
of fish are caught each year from seas and oceans

FISH FARMING

Asia has 87.3 per cent of the world's fishers and fish farmers, but only 68.7 per cent of the global production.

87.3%

68.7%

PRODUCTION RATES PER FISHER

Asia **2.1 tonnes**

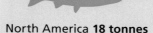
North America **18 tonnes**

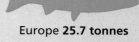
Europe **25.7 tonnes**

FARMING AND FOOD

Farming uses natural plant and animal resources to produce food, materials and even fuel. But even with today's improved techniques, can farmers produce enough to meet increased demand?

Percentage of the world's labour force

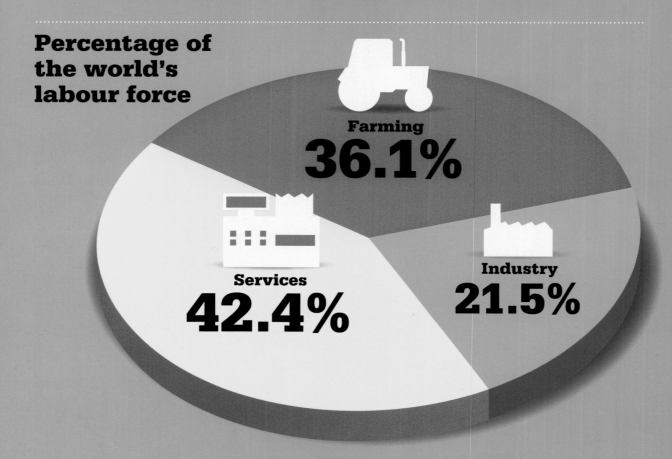

Farming
36.1%

Services
42.4%

Industry
21.5%

FARMERS AND FARM SIZE

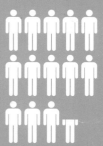

European Union
13.7 million farmers

average farm size
12 hectares

USA
2 million farmers

average farm size
180 hectares

IMPROVED PRODUCTION

In 1960, a single US farmer produced enough food to feed 26 people. Today, that has grown to 155 people. This is due to improvements in farming technology and techniques.

1960

TODAY

Waste

More than **30 per cent** of all food produced on the planet is wasted. That comes to about

1.2-2
BILLION TONNES.

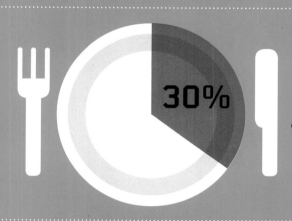

30%

2 billion people could be fed with the amount of food the USA alone throws away each year.

FARM ANIMALS

At present, people around the world use

60,000,000,000

farm animals each year for milk, meat and eggs.

This is set to rise to

120,000,000,000

by 2050.

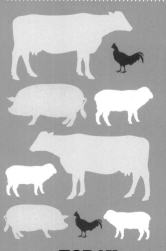

TODAY
(nearly nine for every person)

2050
(nearly 14 for every person)

CLEAN WATER

Water is vital for every living thing – without it, life would not be possible. However, while some people have plenty of water, many others struggle to get enough to survive.

PROBLEMS WITH ACCESS TO CLEAN WATER

Around the world,
780,000,000
people lack access to clean water...

... more than **2.5 times** the population of the USA.

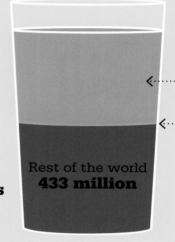

Rest of the world **433 million**

Of these, **343 million** live in Africa,

while just **4 million** live in the Europe AND North America.

2,190 KM

In Africa and Asia, people walk an average distance of nearly 6 km each day to collect water. In a year, the average distance walked is 2,190 km.

Who uses the most?

= 2 litres

Americans use **380 LITRES** of water per day

People living in sub-Saharan Africa use **19 LITRES**

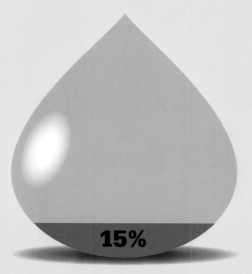

15%

HOW WATER IS USED

Livestock production demands 15 per cent of all the world's irrigation water.

Each year, India uses **70 cubic km** more groundwater than is replaced by rain. Other countries who are using more groundwater than is replenished are:

Pakistan — 35 cubic km
USA — 30 cubic km
China — 30 cubic km

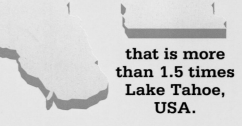

Around the world, an estimated **200 million hours** are spent each day **collecting water.**

DECLINING STOCKS

Underground aquifers are a key source of clean water.

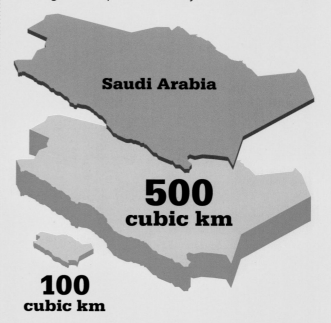

Saudi Arabia

500 cubic km

100 cubic km

When intensive farming started **40 years ago**, there was an estimated **500 cubic km** of water beneath Saudi Arabia. With demand from farming and very little rain, that has now been reduced by **80 per cent** to an estimated **100 cubic km**.

 Globally, the rate of over-use of groundwater is

250 cubic km

that is more than 1.5 times Lake Tahoe, USA.

FORESTS

The world's forests are a key source of many resources, including fuel and building materials. They are also home to many valuable plants and animals that can be used for food and medicines.

SIZE OF FOREST RESOURCES

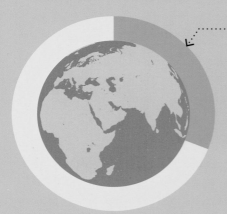

Forests cover **31%** of the world's land area:

4 billion hectares (40 million sq km)

about **6,000 sq metres** for every person

just bigger than the size of a football pitch.

Together, five countries (Russia, Brazil, Canada, USA and China) have more than half of the world's total forest area.

WHAT DO FORESTS PRODUCE?

Global trade in non-wood forest products, such as bamboo, mushrooms, game, fruit, medicinal plants, fibre, gum and resins, is estimated at

US$11,000,000,000

23% of the world's population depend on forests for fuel, food, grazing areas and medicine.

23%

More than 25 per cent of modern medicines originate from tropical forest plants, with an annual value of

US$108 billion.

25%

FORESTS UNDER THREAT

Fires, the expansion of farmland and changes in climate conditions have all been causes in the reduction of the amount of forest land around the world.

Between **1990 and 2000**, the rate of deforestation was

83,000 sq km
per year.

equivalent to an area of **Austria** every year.

Between **2000 and 2010**, the annual rate of deforestation was **52,000 sq km**.

equivalent to the area of **Costa Rica**

This is a decline in the rate of deforestation of nearly

40%

WHO PRODUCES THE MOST FOREST PRODUCTS?

Paper and paperboard

China **26%**

USA **19%**

Germany **6%**

Japan **7%**

Canada **3%**

Rest of the world **39%**

USA **15%**

China **11%**

Canada **10%**

Russia **8%**

Brazil **6%**

Rest of the world **50%**

Sawn wood

METALS AND MINERALS

Many resources, including minerals and metals, lie buried deep beneath the ground. Getting them to the surface involves some of the biggest machines and vehicles ever built.

HOW ARE MINERALS MINED?

Different mining techniques are used depending on where the resources are buried and the type of rock above them.

MOUNTAIN TOP
The entire top of a hill or mountain is removed to reach the minerals beneath.

CONTOUR
The rock lying above the minerals and running around the contours of a hill is removed.

OPEN-PIT AND STRIP MINES
A large area of rock is stripped clear to reach the minerals buried beneath.

DRIFT MINE
A horizontal tunnel is cut directly into the rock to reach minerals.

There are **60** different **minerals** found in a single **computer chip**, including **silicon, copper, gold** and **tin.**

How minerals are combined and altered
How iron ore is turned into steel

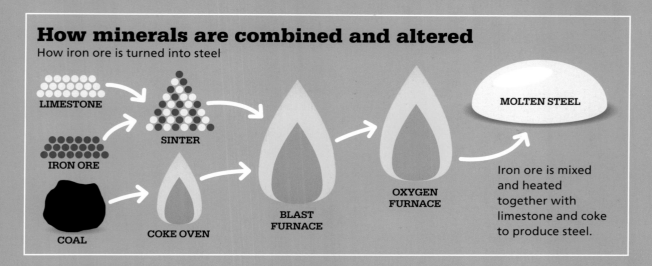

LIMESTONE

SINTER

IRON ORE

COAL

COKE OVEN

BLAST FURNACE

OXYGEN FURNACE

MOLTEN STEEL

Iron ore is mixed and heated together with limestone and coke to produce steel.

PRODUCTION LEVELS AND USES

Copper 17 million tonnes — Used in cables, pipes, roofing

Gold 2,700 tonnes — Used in jewellery, dentistry, medicine

Lead 5.2 million tonnes — Used in roofing

Platinum 179 tonnes • Used in jewellery, electrical equipment

Zinc 13 million tonnes — Used in galvanising and protecting metals, coins

World mineral production

URANIUM
Uranium is used in nuclear reactors to produce electricity.

 = =

1 TONNE URANIUM

16,000 TONNES OF COAL

40 MILLION KILOWATT HOURS OF ELECTRICITY

SLOPE MINE
A sloping tunnel leads down to minerals buried underground.

SHAFT MINE
Long shafts are dug straight down to reach minerals far underground. ....>

Aluminium
is one of the most abundant metal elements in the Earth's crust, and this is how it is used....

machinery 8%

transport 37%

building 13%

other 11%

electrical 8%

packaging 23%

COAL

This fossil fuel is formed from the remains of plants that died millions of years ago. It is burned in homes for heat, or in power stations to produce electricity.

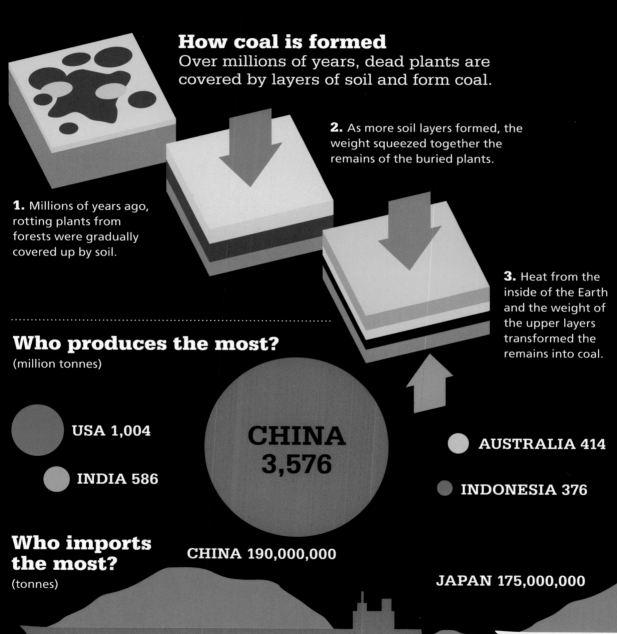

How coal is formed
Over millions of years, dead plants are covered by layers of soil and form coal.

1. Millions of years ago, rotting plants from forests were gradually covered up by soil.

2. As more soil layers formed, the weight squeezed together the remains of the buried plants.

3. Heat from the inside of the Earth and the weight of the upper layers transformed the remains into coal.

Who produces the most?
(million tonnes)

USA 1,004

INDIA 586

CHINA 3,576

AUSTRALIA 414

INDONESIA 376

Who imports the most?
(tonnes)

CHINA 190,000,000

JAPAN 175,000,000

GERMANY 41,000,000

CHINESE TAIPEI 66,000,000

HOW MUCH COAL IS LEFT?

It is estimated that there are more than **3 trillion tonnes** of coal left in the USA...

... only about **235 billion tonnes** of this can be mined using present-day technology.

If coal production grows at its present rate, this will be exhausted in less than 170 years.

20%
of global greenhouse gas emissions

Side effects of using coal
While burning coal produces energy for heating and generates electricity, it also releases greenhouse gases. These are thought to be a major cause of global warming.

WHO HAS THE MOST COAL?
(world coal reserves)

USA 27.5%

Russia 18.3%

Europe and Eurasia 17.2%

China 13.3%

Africa 3.7%

India 7.0%

Central and South America 0.9%

Australia and NZ 8.9%

● Rest of the World 3.2%

SOUTH KOREA 129,000,000

UK 33,000,000

INDIA 105,000,000

NATURAL GAS

Like coal, natural gas is a fossil fuel that is burned in power stations to produce electricity. This non-renewable fuel is also piped into homes, where it is used for heating and cooking.

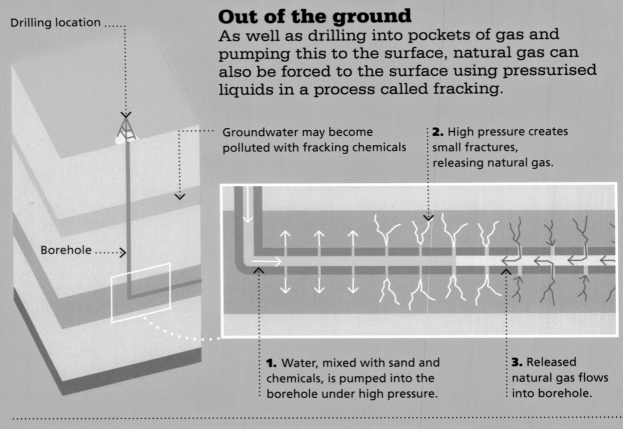

Drilling location ......

Out of the ground

As well as drilling into pockets of gas and pumping this to the surface, natural gas can also be forced to the surface using pressurised liquids in a process called fracking.

Groundwater may become polluted with fracking chemicals

2. High pressure creates small fractures, releasing natural gas.

Borehole ......>

1. Water, mixed with sand and chemicals, is pumped into the borehole under high pressure.

3. Released natural gas flows into borehole.

WHAT NATURAL GAS IS USED FOR

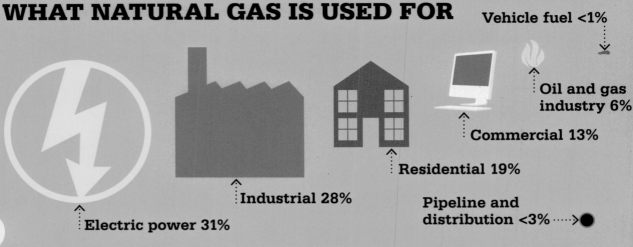

Vehicle fuel <1%

Oil and gas industry 6%

Commercial 13%

Residential 19%

Industrial 28%

Electric power 31%

Pipeline and distribution <3% ····>●

Who produces the most
(billion cubic metres)

RUSSIA
677

USA
651

CANADA
160

QATAR
151

IRAN
149

NATURAL GAS FACTS

Natural gas is odourless and colourless.
Gas companies add a substance called mercaptan, which smells like rotten eggs, so that gas leaks are noticeable.

To transport it, natural gas is chilled to about -160°C, when it turns into a liquid.

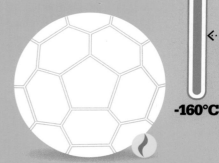

0.0°C Melting point of water

-89.2°C Lowest recorded temperature on Earth (Vostok Station, Antarctica)

-160°C

It becomes 600 times smaller. This is the same as shrinking a football down to a marble with a diameter of about 2.6 cm.

Who uses the most
(billion cubic metres)

USA
683.3

EU
515

IRAN
137.5

CHINA
129

RUSSIA
414.1

OIL

Crude oil is usually formed from the bodies of tiny dead organisms, such as plankton and algae. These were buried millions of years ago. Pressure and high temperature then turned them into oil.

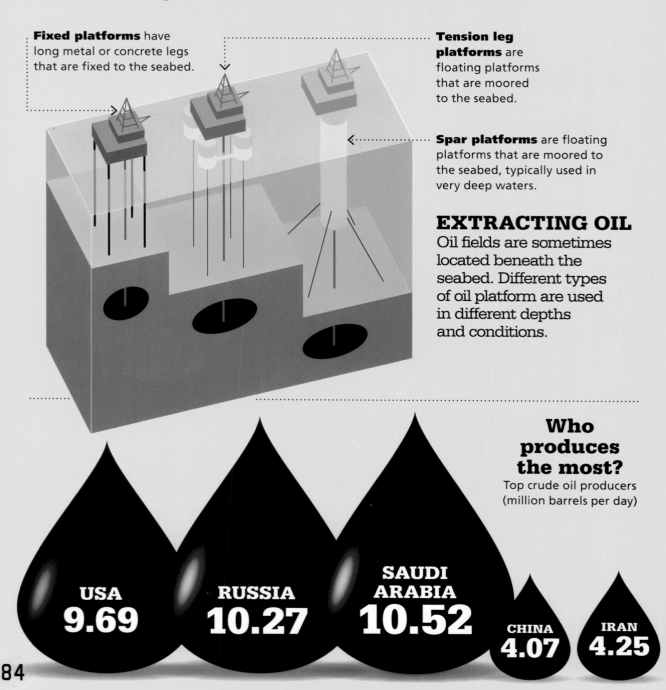

Fixed platforms have long metal or concrete legs that are fixed to the seabed.

Tension leg platforms are floating platforms that are moored to the seabed.

Spar platforms are floating platforms that are moored to the seabed, typically used in very deep waters.

EXTRACTING OIL

Oil fields are sometimes located beneath the seabed. Different types of oil platform are used in different depths and conditions.

Who produces the most?

Top crude oil producers (million barrels per day)

USA
9.69

RUSSIA
10.27

SAUDI ARABIA
10.52

CHINA
4.07

IRAN
4.25

WHAT CRUDE OIL IS TURNED INTO

A **159 litre** barrel of crude oil makes about **170 litres** of petroleum products:

Heavy fuel oil **3.8 litres**

Other distillates (heating oil) **3.8 litres**

Liquid Petroleum Gas (LPG) **7.6 litres**

Jet fuel **15.1 litres**

Other products **26.3 litres**

Diesel **41.5 litres**

Petrol **71.9 litres**

OTHER PRODUCTS INCLUDE ink, crayons, dishwashing liquids, deodorant, eyeglasses, CDs and DVDs, tyres, ammonia and heart valves.

HOW MUCH IS USED?

Every day, Americans use on average about

136 billion litres of petrol.

The USA uses **18.9 million** barrels of crude oil **every day.**

Top exporters

(million barrels per day)

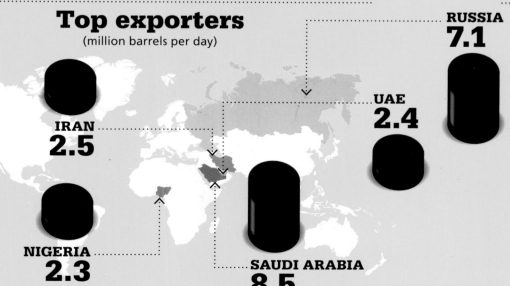

RUSSIA 7.1

UAE 2.4

IRAN 2.5

NIGERIA 2.3

SAUDI ARABIA 8.5

WATER POWER

Renewable resources are those that can be used over and over again. Flowing water in rivers and the sea has been used as a power source for thousands of years.

HOW MUCH POWER IS PRODUCED

Hydroelectric power provides **20 per cent** of the entire world's electricity.

Other sources 80%

Hydroelectric

World's biggest producers
(percentage of world total)

CHINA 19.8

BRAZIL 12.3

CANADA 10.8

USA 9.4

Between them, the USA, China, Canada and Brazil produced more than **50 per cent** of the world's hydroelectric electricity.

THREE GORGES DAM

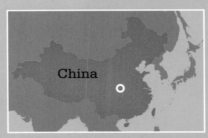

The Three Gorges Dam in China is one of the biggest hydroelectric power stations in the world.

Weight of the water (estimated at more than 300 million tonnes) may cause earthquakes in the area.

cost to build:

US$37 BILLION

Generates 11 times as much electricity as the Hoover Dam, USA.

Relocated 1.3 million people (13 cities, 140 towns, and 1,350 villages)

Three Gorges Dam **186 M**

Washington monument **169 M**

Taller than the Washington monument and **2 KM WIDE**

HYDROELECTRIC DAM

A dam creates a large lake from which water can be channelled past bladed wheels called turbines, sending them spinning. The turbines are connected to generators, which produce electricity.

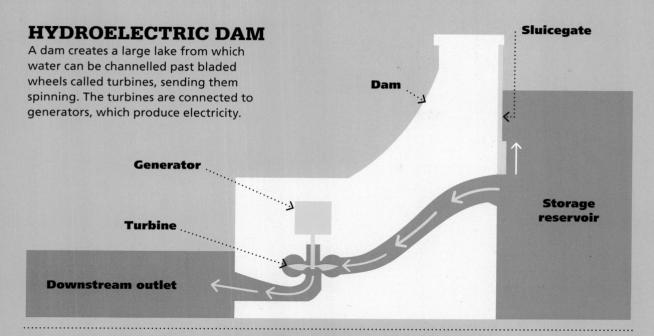

Sluicegate

Dam

Generator

Turbine

Downstream outlet

Storage reservoir

TIDAL POWER STATIONS

Every day, the world's seas and oceans rise and fall with the tides. This movement can be harnessed to produce electricity.

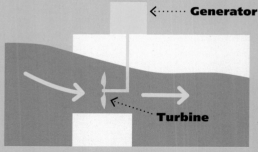

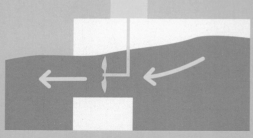

Generator

Turbine

1. As the tide comes in, the flowing water spins turbines. The turbines are connected to generators to produce electricity.

2. The same thing happens when the tide goes out. The water may flow the other way, but the turbine still spins and the generator still produces electricity.

HOW WAVE POWER WORKS

This generator uses the movement of waves to produce electricity. Experimental and working wave generators can be found off the coasts of the USA, UK, Australia and Sweden.

Jointed parts rock up and down as the waves move past. This movement is used to generate power.

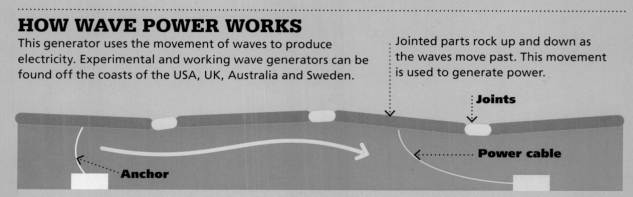

Joints

Power cable

Anchor

WIND POWER

Early windmills used the power of the wind to pump water and grind crops to make flour. Today, huge wind farms with thousands of turbines produce power for millions of people.

HOW MODERN WIND TURBINES WORK

Wind turbines catch the wind using tall, propeller-like blades. These are connected to a generator, which produces electricity as the blades spin.

Turbine blade

Gearbox transfers spinning movement to the generator.

Generator produces electricity as the blades spin around.

Main shaft spins around with the blades.

GRINDING CROPS

Traditional windmills used large sails to catch the wind, sending them spinning. This movement was transferred to huge millstones, which ground crops between them to produce flour.

Windmill sails

Cogs and shafts turned by the wind

Flour

Millstones

Denmark generates nearly **20 per cent** of its electricity supply using more than **5,000** wind turbines – nearly one turbine for every **1,000** Danish people.

TURBINE TYPES

There are two main types of wind turbine. Horizontal axis turbines have the main shaft arranged horizontally, while vertical axis turbines have their shafts arranged vertically.

Horizontal axis

Vertical axis

The world's largest windfarm,

the Horse Hollow Wind Energy Center in Texas, USA, has

421

wind turbines and generates enough electricity to power

220,000

homes per year.

Tower holds the blades high. The turbine can rotate so that the blades face into the wind.

How much power is produced using the wind?
(megawatts)

INDIA 18,421

SPAIN 22,796

GERMANY 31,332

USA 60,007

CHINA 75,564

SOLAR POWER

Every hour, the Sun beams more than enough energy at the Earth to meet global demand for a whole year. However, the amount that can be used to produce electricity depends on where you live.

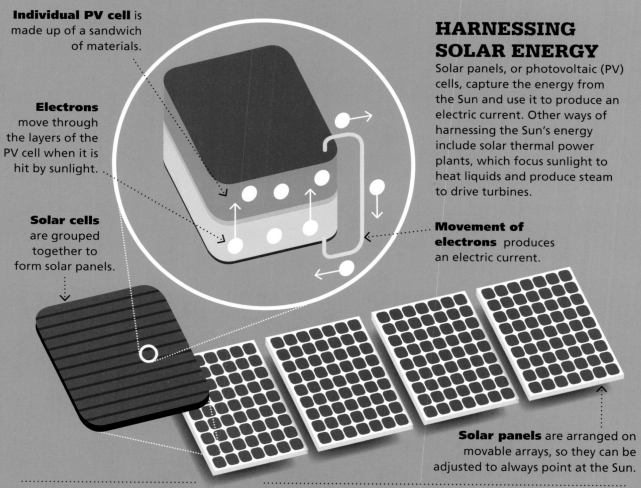

Individual PV cell is made up of a sandwich of materials.

Electrons move through the layers of the PV cell when it is hit by sunlight.

Solar cells are grouped together to form solar panels.

HARNESSING SOLAR ENERGY

Solar panels, or photovoltaic (PV) cells, capture the energy from the Sun and use it to produce an electric current. Other ways of harnessing the Sun's energy include solar thermal power plants, which focus sunlight to heat liquids and produce steam to drive turbines.

Movement of electrons produces an electric current.

Solar panels are arranged on movable arrays, so they can be adjusted to always point at the Sun.

HOW MUCH POWER CAN BE PRODUCED?

One of the world's largest solar thermal power plants is in Andalusia, Spain.

Spain

COVERS AN AREA EQUIVALENT TO

210 football pitches

it uses **600,000** mirrors

it generates **150 megawatts** of electricity – enough for a city of **500,000**

One of the biggest solar PV power stations in the world in Gujarat, India, produces

600 MEGAWATTS

enough to supply the power for nearly **400,000** homes in the USA.

On a sunny day at noon, each square metre of the Earth's surface receives around

1 kilowatt

of solar power – the equivalent power used by a fridge.

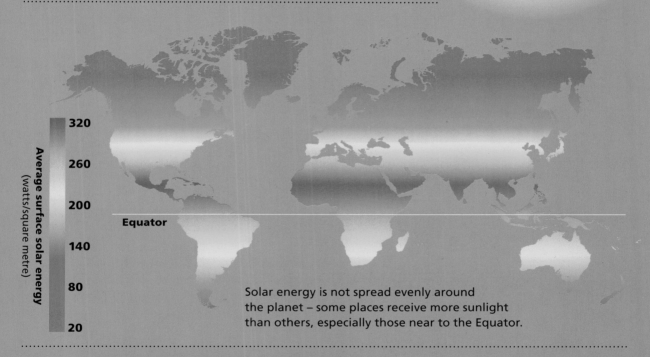

Average surface solar energy (watts/square metre)

320

260

200

Equator

140

80

20

Solar energy is not spread evenly around the planet – some places receive more sunlight than others, especially those near to the Equator.

88.738 km/h

Solar cells

The record speed for a solar powered car is 88.738 km/h set by Sunswift IV in Australia on 7 January 2011.

OTHER RENEWABLES

Renewable sources of energy also include plant and animal products, as well as harnessing the enormous amounts of heat produced at the Earth's core.

GEOTHERMAL ENERGY

Temperatures beneath the Earth's surface increase as you get closer to the planet's core. Things become so hot, that rock melts and flows as a superhot runny liquid. By drilling down through the Earth's crust, this energy can be used to heat water, producing steam to power turbines and produce electricity.

Core
4,900–
6,100°C

Outer core
4,500–
5,500°C

Surface
15°C

0°C

Surface

Outer core

Core

Cross-section of the Earth

Geothermal power plants are built in areas where the Earth's heat rises close to the surface.

4. Steam is used to spin turbines, which are connected to generators to produce electricity.

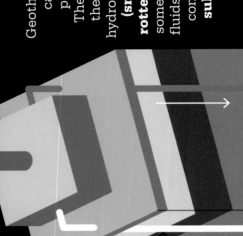

HOW CLEAN IS GEOTHERMAL ENERGY?

Geothermal power plants produce less than 1 per cent of the carbon dioxide emissions of a fossil fuel plant...

1%

97%

...and emit 97 per cent fewer sulphur compounds than fossil fuel plants. Sulphur compounds are the cause of acid rain.

Geothermal plants can cause problems. These include the release of hydrogen sulphide **(smells like rotten eggs)** and some geothermal fluids, which may contain **toxic substances.**

1. Water is pumped down through boreholes.

2. Hot rocks heat the water, producing steam.

3. Steam rises back to the surface through boreholes.

Biggest producers of wood fuel

India 16%

China 10%

Brazil 8%

Ethiopia 5%

Biofuels

Most of the energy on our planet comes from the Sun. Plants use this solar energy to produce food for themselves and for other living things to eat. These energy stores can be used and converted into biofuels, such as wood, methane and ethanol.

Sun

Plants

Animals

Methane (gas)

Wood (solid)

Sugar

Ethanol (liquid)

Chlorophyll

Photosynthesis

Chlorophyll is found inside many plant cells. It plays an important part in photosynthesis, where the Sun's energy is used to produce sugars. The sugars in some crops, including corn and sugar cane, can be refined to produce biofuels, such as ethanol.

ORDER OF LIVING THINGS

Our planet is teeming with billions of organisms, from microscopic algae to gigantic whales. In order to identify each living thing, scientists use a classification system.

KINGDOMS

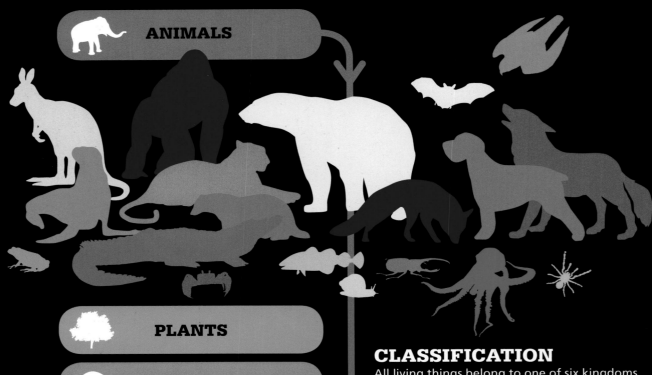

ANIMALS

PLANTS

FUNGI

PROTISTS
(MICRO-ORGANISMS)

EUBACTERIA
(MICRO-ORGANISMS)

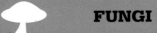

ARCHEOBACTERIA
(MICRO-ORGANISMS)

CLASSIFICATION

All living things belong to one of six kingdoms. Each kingdom is divided into groups, from phylum down to species. The graphic shows how a species, in this case the wolf, is identified using this classification system.

INSECTS OUTNUMBER HUMANS BY
200,000,000 TO 1

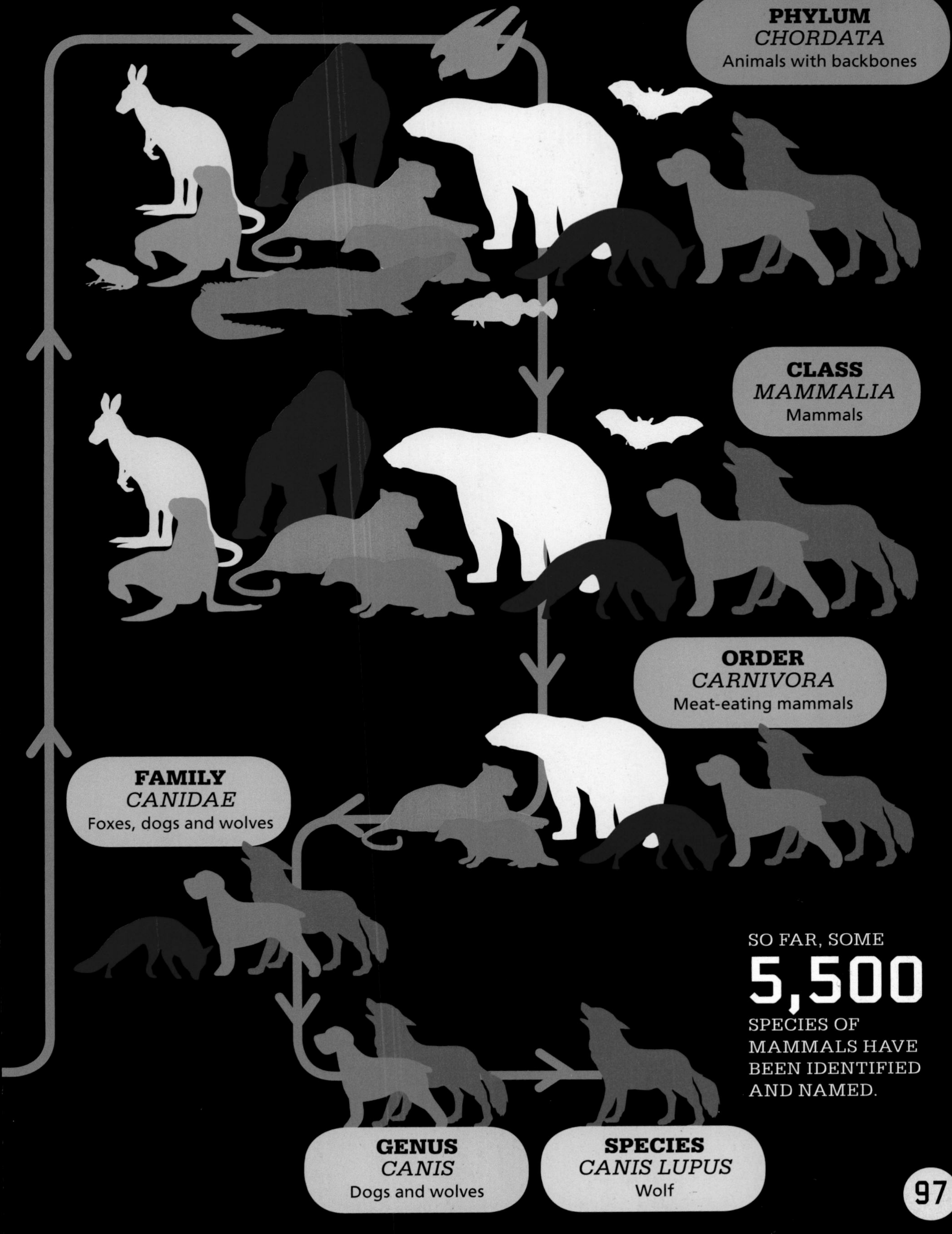

PHYLUM
CHORDATA
Animals with backbones

CLASS
MAMMALIA
Mammals

ORDER
CARNIVORA
Meat-eating mammals

FAMILY
CANIDAE
Foxes, dogs and wolves

SO FAR, SOME
5,500
SPECIES OF
MAMMALS HAVE
BEEN IDENTIFIED
AND NAMED.

GENUS
CANIS
Dogs and wolves

SPECIES
CANIS LUPUS
Wolf

MICROSCOPIC WORLD

There are entire kingdoms of micro-organisms that are too small to see with the naked eye. For example, a single gram of soil can contain 40 million bacteria alone!

BIGGEST KILLERS

The number of people killed each year by various diseases caused by micro-organisms.

3.9 MILLION
LOWER RESPIRATORY INFECTIONS (SUCH AS PNEUMONIA)

2.8 MILLION
HIV/AIDS

1.8 MILLION
DIARRHEAL DISEASES

1.6 MILLION
TB

1.3 MILLION
MALARIA

0.6 MILLION
MEASLES

BREAD

Not all micro-organisms are harmful. Humans use some in food and drink and to treat waste. For example, yeast is used in bread-making to turn the sugars in bread dough into tiny bubbles of carbon dioxide, making the bread 'rise'.

400 NANOMETRES

The size of the largest viruses – about 1/250th the width of a human hair.

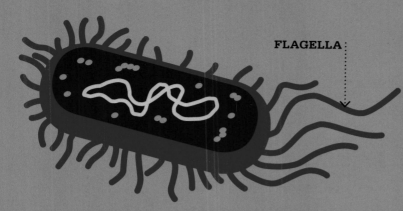

FLAGELLA

CELLS

All organisms are made up of cells. Micro-organisms often consist of one cell, while plants and animals are made up of billions. Prokaryotic cells are those that do not contain a cell nucleus. They include bacteria, some of which have flagella, which they wiggle to move about.

NUCLEUS

NUCLEUS

PLANT CELL

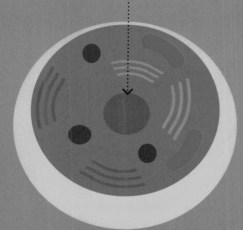

EUKARYOTIC

Eukaryotic cells contain a cell nucleus, inside which is the genetic information for the cell. Plants and animals are formed from two different types of eukaryotic cells.

ANIMAL CELL

About 10,000 human cells could fit onto the head of a pin

10,000

THE LARGEST KNOWN CELLS ARE UNFERTILISED OSTRICH EGGS.

They weigh about 1.6 kg – nearly two bags of sugar.

CHICKEN EGG

ALLIGATOR EGG

TURTLE EGG

HUMMINGBIRD EGG

ENERGY PRODUCTION

The Sun is the source of most of the energy used on our planet. Plants convert this energy into substances that all living things can then use to produce energy to survive and grow.

LIGHT ENERGY FROM THE SUN

CHLOROPHYLL

WATER

CARBON DIOXIDE

PHOTOSYNTHESIS

Chlorophyll is found inside many plant cells. It plays an important part in harnessing sunlight during a process called photosynthesis. This process converts water and the gas carbon dioxide into sugars and oxygen.

WITH OR WITHOUT

Respiration that uses oxygen is called aerobic, while respiration that does not use oxygen is called anaerobic.

OXYGEN

SUGAR

EACH YEAR, ONE HECTARE OF TREES CONSUMES THE SAME AMOUNT OF CARBON DIOXIDE PRODUCED BY AN AVERAGE CAR THAT HAS BEEN DRIVEN FOR

100,000 KM

That same hectare of trees also produces enough oxygen for

45

people to breathe for a year.

RESPIRATION

During respiration, sugars are used to produce energy. Tiny structures called mitochondria found in cells are the main sites for this energy production. As well as producing energy, this process also creates the gas carbon dioxide and water.

MITOCHONDRIA

CELL DIVISION

Every organism contains instructions that determine how it looks and behaves. These instructions are stored on a long, twisted molecule called DNA.

BASE PAIR

CYTOSINE   GUANINE

ADENINE   THYMINE

PHOSPHATE
BACKBONE

DNA MOLECULE

A DNA molecule consists of two twisting backbones, which are joined together by chemicals that are linked in pairs, called base pairs. These pairs are organised into certain sequences, called genes, and these determine how an organism acts.

There are an estimated 3 billion DNA bases in the human genome

3,000,000,000

CHROMOSOMES

Chromosomes are structures found inside cells. They are made up of long strands of DNA that are twisted and coiled together tightly.

If it was unravelled, the **DNA** from a single **cell** in a **human body** would be approximately **2 metres** long – that's taller than most humans!

CELL DIVISION

Cells divide in order to multiply. To do this, they need to duplicate their genetic information before splitting apart.

HUMANS AND CHIMPS SHARE UP TO

95%

OF THEIR DNA

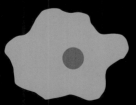

1. PARENT CELL

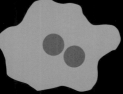

2. NUCLEUS DIVIDES

3. CELL SPLITS

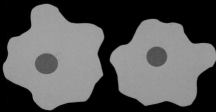

4. TWO DAUGHTER CELLS

REPRODUCTION

All living things reproduce, so that their species can survive. Reproduction can be asexual, whereby one organism duplicates itself, or sexual, whereby cells from two organisms join together to produce young.

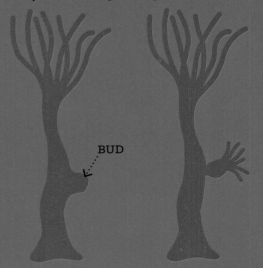

BUD

ASEXUAL REPRODUCTION

Some simple organisms, such as amoeba, will simply divide in two. Others, such as this hydra, reproduce by budding, creating an identical, but smaller, version of themselves.

FLOWERS AND SEEDS

Plants contain male cells, called pollen, stored in anthers, and female cells inside an ovary. The two cells join together to form seeds. Some seeds, such as the pips in an apple, are surrounded by fruit. Animals eat the fruit and the seeds are spread in the animals' dung. Sycamore seeds have a special wing shape, which allows them to spin away from the parent plant and spread.

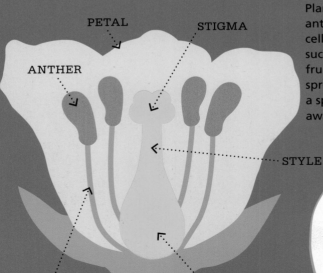

PETAL

STIGMA

ANTHER

STYLE

FILAMENT

OVARY

SEED WINGS

SYCAMORE SEEDS

APPLE SEEDS

FRUIT

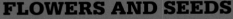

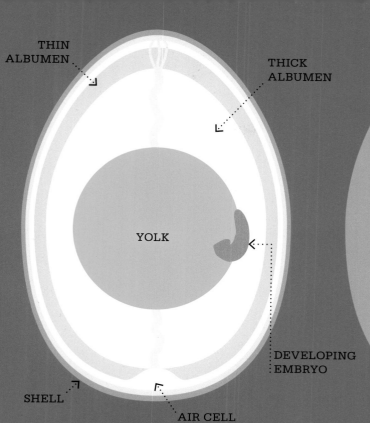

THIN ALBUMEN

THICK ALBUMEN

YOLK

DEVELOPING EMBRYO

SHELL

AIR CELL

LAYING EGGS

Many animals lay eggs which contain the developing young. Inside a chicken's egg, the developing young, or embryo, is fed by nutrients in the yolk, while being supported and protected by the albumen.

FEMALE ELEPHANT **3,000 KG**

LIVE BIRTH

The young of mammals develop inside the mother's uterus. This development period is called the gestation. Over time, the young will develop and grow until they are old enough to be born.

22 MONTHS

GESTATION PERIOD FOR AN ELEPHANT – THE LONGEST OF ANY LAND ANIMAL.

CALF
105 KG

RABBITS HAVE A FAST BREEDING RATE. IN A SINGLE BREEDING SEASON, A PAIR CAN MULTIPLY TO AS MANY AS

800

RABBITS OVER THREE OR FOUR GENERATIONS.

GROWING UP

As a plant or animal gets older, it grows and matures before it finally dies. During its life span, it may go through many stages, including a complete change in body shape and form.

HOW LONG CAN ANIMALS LIVE?

ANT 6 MONTHS

MOUSE 4 YEARS

RABBIT 10 YEARS

LIFE CYCLES

Some animals, including butterflies, change completely as they mature. This process is called metamorphosis. Mammals, such as horses, keep the same body shape, but grow larger.

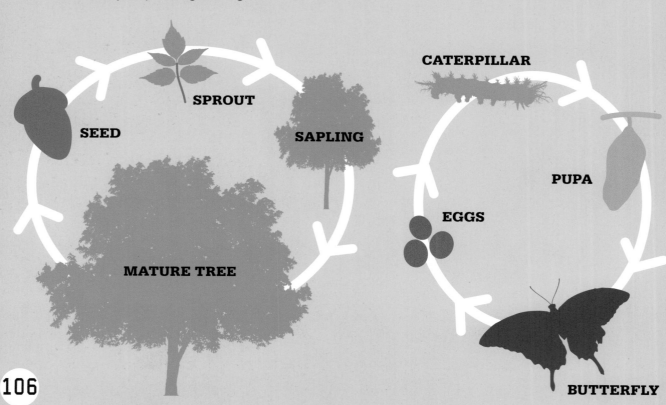

SEED

SPROUT

SAPLING

MATURE TREE

CATERPILLAR

PUPA

EGGS

BUTTERFLY

A **Great Basin Bristlecone pine** in North America is the **oldest** known living individual tree. Samples from its core and rings show that it is more than **4,800 years old.**

BOTTLENOSE DOLPHIN
45 YEARS

HORSE
30 YEARS

KOI CARP
70 YEARS

ASIAN ELEPHANT
60 YEARS

HUMAN
70–80 YEARS

GALAPAGOS TORTOISE
190 YEARS

YEARLING

HORSE

FOAL

4,265

A type of black coral called Leiopathes is one of the oldest continuously living organisms. Some specimens of the coral are around 4,265 years old.

FOOD WEBS

Most energy comes from the Sun. This energy is harnessed by plants and passed on when they are eaten by animals, who are, in turn, eaten by their predators. This relationship is called a food chain.

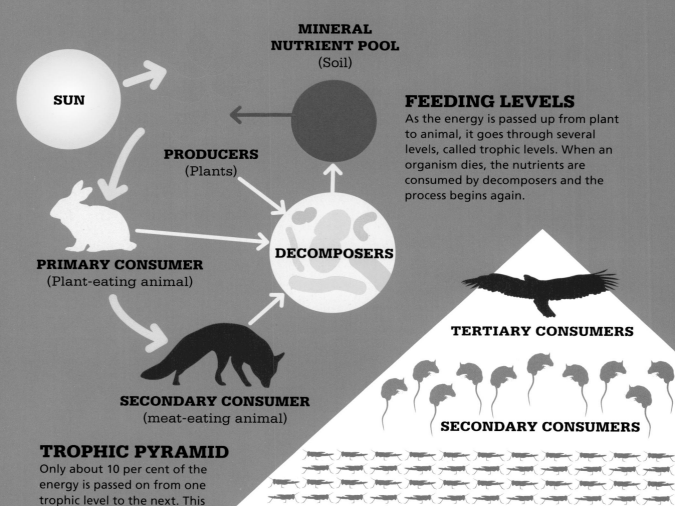

MINERAL NUTRIENT POOL
(Soil)

SUN

PRODUCERS
(Plants)

DECOMPOSERS

PRIMARY CONSUMER
(Plant-eating animal)

SECONDARY CONSUMER
(meat-eating animal)

FEEDING LEVELS

As the energy is passed up from plant to animal, it goes through several levels, called trophic levels. When an organism dies, the nutrients are consumed by decomposers and the process begins again.

TERTIARY CONSUMERS

SECONDARY CONSUMERS

PRIMARY CONSUMERS

PRODUCERS

TROPHIC PYRAMID

Only about 10 per cent of the energy is passed on from one trophic level to the next. This means that there are fewer living things the higher up the trophic levels you go, creating a trophic pyramid.

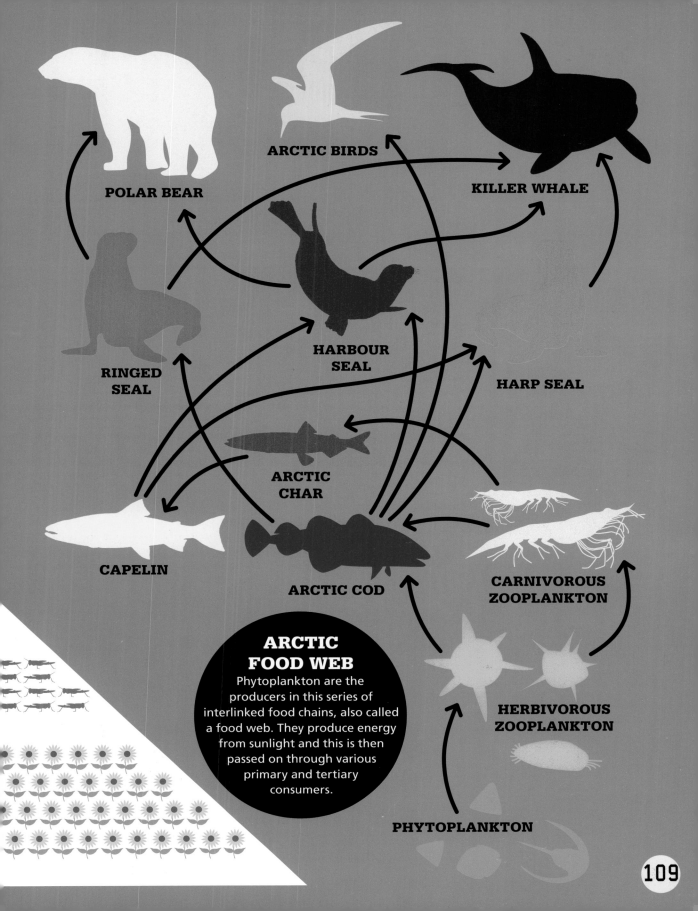

POLAR BEAR

ARCTIC BIRDS

KILLER WHALE

RINGED SEAL

HARBOUR SEAL

HARP SEAL

ARCTIC CHAR

CAPELIN

ARCTIC COD

CARNIVOROUS ZOOPLANKTON

HERBIVOROUS ZOOPLANKTON

PHYTOPLANKTON

ARCTIC FOOD WEB

Phytoplankton are the producers in this series of interlinked food chains, also called a food web. They produce energy from sunlight and this is then passed on through various primary and tertiary consumers.

EVOLUTION

Throughout the history of the Earth, new species have appeared while others have died out or changed. This process is called evolution and it occurs in response to changing conditions on our planet.

98%

2%

1800

95%

5%

1900

MOTH
The peppered moth has changed as its habitat has altered. During the 19th century, pollution from factories darkened tree barks. This meant that light versions of the moth were easy to spot by predators. Dark varieties made up a tiny amount of peppered moths at the start of the 19th century. By 1900, they made up more than 95 per cent.

EXTINCTION
When a species dies out it becomes extinct. There have been several periods when a lot of species died out – these are called mass extinction events. This graphic shows rates of species extinction – the taller the peak the more species died out. Mass extinctions have a wide range of causes, including massive volcanic activity, sudden climate change and asteroid impacts.

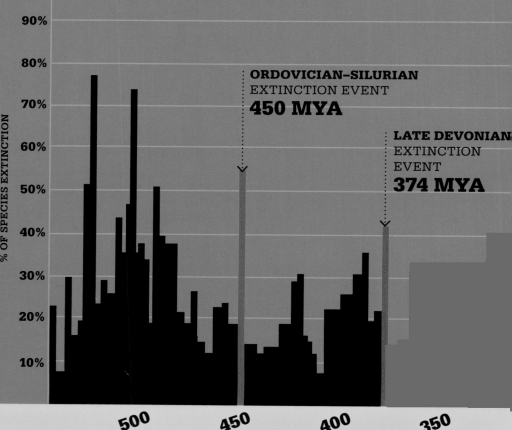

ORDOVICIAN–SILURIAN
EXTINCTION EVENT
450 MYA

LATE DEVONIAN
EXTINCTION EVENT
374 MYA

% OF SPECIES EXTINCTION

100%
90%
80%
70%
60%
50%
40%
30%
20%
10%

MILLIONS OF YEARS AGO (MYA)

500   450   400   350

FINCHES

British scientist Charles Darwin developed the theory of evolution by studying animal life on the Galapagos Islands in the Pacific. Here, he noticed that various species of finches had differently shaped beaks to suit the types of food they ate.

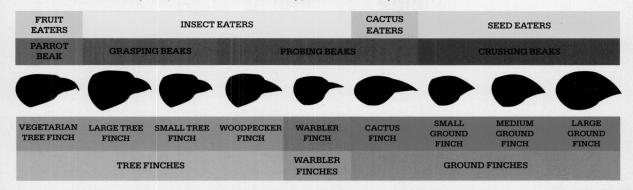

FRUIT EATERS	INSECT EATERS				CACTUS EATERS	SEED EATERS		
PARROT BEAK	GRASPING BEAKS			PROBING BEAKS		CRUSHING BEAKS		
VEGETARIAN TREE FINCH	LARGE TREE FINCH	SMALL TREE FINCH	WOODPECKER FINCH	WARBLER FINCH	CACTUS FINCH	SMALL GROUND FINCH	MEDIUM GROUND FINCH	LARGE GROUND FINCH
TREE FINCHES				WARBLER FINCHES	GROUND FINCHES			

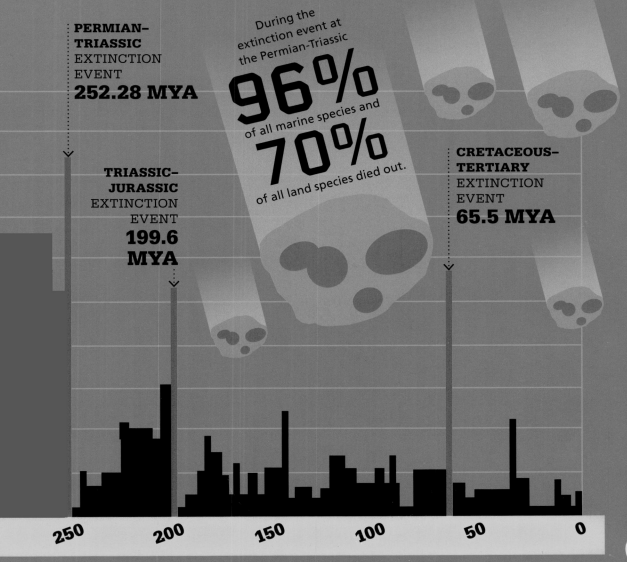

PERMIAN–TRIASSIC EXTINCTION EVENT **252.28 MYA**

TRIASSIC–JURASSIC EXTINCTION EVENT **199.6 MYA**

During the extinction event at the Permian-Triassic **96%** of all marine species and **70%** of all land species died out.

CRETACEOUS–TERTIARY EXTINCTION EVENT **65.5 MYA**

250   200   150   100   50   0

FAST AND SLOW

Living beings often use speed for survival, for example to outrun a predator. Other organisms live at a slower pace in order to save energy.

The fastest accelerating living thing on the planet is the hat thrower fungus. The spores are released on a jet of liquid with an acceleration of

0–32 KM/H IN JUST 2 MILLIONTHS OF A SECOND

experiencing forces of 20,000G – astronauts blasting into space only experience 4G.

FASTEST ANIMALS

PEREGRINE FALCON
320 KM/H

SPEED

AUSTRALIAN TIGER BEETLES

CAN REACH SPEEDS OF 6.7 KM/H WHEN ESCAPING PREDATORS. BUT THEY ARE ONLY 1 CM LONG, SO THEY TRAVEL AT ABOUT

170 BODY LENGTHS PER SECOND.

IF AN OLYMPIC SPRINTER COULD MATCH THAT RATE OF BODY LENGTHS PER SECOND, THEY WOULD BE RUNNING AT NEARLY

1,200 KM/H
– THAT'S FASTER THAN THE SPEED OF SOUND AT SEA LEVEL!

SLOWEST ANIMALS

GARDEN SNAIL
0.03 KM/H

GIANT TORTOISE
0.3 KM/H

IN ONE MINUTE A GARDEN SNAIL CAN TRAVEL

5 CM

SEAHORSE
0.02 KM/H

IN ONE HOUR THEY CAN GROW 4 CM

Some species of bamboo are the fastest growing plants in the world, capable of growing 1 metre in a single day.

SWORDFISH AND MARLIN
100 KM/H
FASTEST FISH

HORSE
70 KM/H

HUMAN SPRINTER
37.5 KM/H

CHEETAH 120 KM/H
FASTEST LAND ANIMAL

WOLF 65 KM/H

AT THIS SPEED, THE AUSTRALIAN TIGER BEETLE WOULD COMPLETE 100 METRES IN JUST

0.3 SECONDS.

AN OLYMPIC SPRINTER TAKES
10 SECONDS TO RUN 100 METRES.

BIG AND SMALL

Whether they reach super-size proportions or can pass through the eye of a needle, these record-breaking organisms have found their own way of surviving in the world.

A **giant fungus** of the honey mushroom species covers **8.9 sq km** of land in Oregon, USA, making it the **largest** ever known organism by area.

GIRAFFE 6 M

Standing next to some of the tallest animals in the world, the average human is a little short. Top of the tree are giraffes, which can reach more than three times an average person's height.

OSTRICH 2.75 M

ELEPHANT 4 M

MAN 1.8 M

HORSE 2.2 M

THE BLUE WHALE IS THE LARGEST ANIMAL EVER.

IT CAN WEIGH UP TO
200 TONNES
ABOUT THE WEIGHT OF 40 ELEPHANTS, OR 15 BUSES.

30 M LONG

Which is about the same length as 17 people, 3 school buses or a basketball court.

It can eat up to 3.5 tonnes of krill in a day.

ITS TONGUE CAN WEIGH AS MUCH AS AN ELEPHANT.

A newborn blue whale puts on about 90 kg of weight every single day during its first year.

SMALLEST FLOWERING PLANT
GENUS WOLFFIA
An individual plant is just 0.6 mm long and 0.3 mm wide.

ACTUAL SIZE

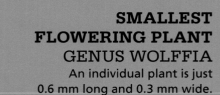

BIGGEST FLOWER
RAFFLESIA ARNOLDII
It measures up to 1 metre across and gives off an odour of decaying flesh.

CAMEL 2.15 M

Sequoia 115 m

TALLEST TREE

29 Elephants

GREATEST JUMPER

The froghopper is the world's greatest jumper. It can leap 70 cm into the air, but it's only 0.6 cm long.

THAT IS THE SAME AS A PERSON LEAPING OVER A 210-METRE HIGH SKYSCRAPER!

RECORD BREAKERS

The creatures on these pages have developed some amazing ways of surviving, whether it is super-strength, deep-sea diving or living together in enormous groups.

STRONGEST

Gram for gram, the world's strongest creature is thought to be the rhinoceros beetle. It can lift 850 times its own body weight.

That's equivalent to a human lifting

60 TONNES!

ANT FACTS

In the Brazilian rainforest, the biomass of ants is roughly four times greater than that of all of the land vertebrates in the rainforest combined.

Although ants make up 2 per cent of all known insect species, they form at least one-third of all insect biomass.

The largest known swarm of locusts was made up of 40 billion insects and covered 1,036 square kilometres – that's the same size as the island of Tahiti.

40,000,000,000

The
**GOLIATH
BIRD-EATING
SPIDER**
has a leg span of up to

30 CM

and is the largest spider by mass.

Argentine ants live in enormous **mega-colonies**, one of which stretches for **6,000 km** along the Mediterranean Coast.

HUMAN FREE
DIVER
214 м

EMPEROR
PENGUIN
550 м

LEATHERBACK
TURTLE
1,280 м

ELEPHANT SEAL
1,500 м

DEEP DIVERS

SPERM WHALE
3,000 м

FORMATION
OF EARTH
**4.5 BILLION
YEARS AGO**

ANIMAL COUNTDOWN

Over billions of years, life on Earth has evolved from simple single-celled organisms into a wide range of complex creatures. On the way, new forms of life have appeared, while others have become extinct.

**1.5
BILLION
YEARS
AGO**

The Cambrian Explosion, about **540 MYA** saw an enormous expansion in life forms, including the evolution of **chordates** (animals with a backbone or notochord).

COMPLEX CELLS
**2 BILLION
YEARS AGO**

Oldest fossils

The oldest fossils ever discovered were formed 3.4 billion years ago. They are the remains of ancient cells that lived at a time when the Earth was far warmer than today and its surface was covered with active volcanoes.

MULTICELLULAR LIFE
1 BILLION YEARS AGO

3.5 BILLION YEARS AGO

3 BILLION YEARS AGO

EVOLUTION OF PROKARYOTES
3.8 BILLION YEARS AGO

2.5 BILLION YEARS AGO

23:59

If the entire history of the Earth was condensed into just one single day, then modern humans would appear at one minute to midnight!

INSECTS
400 MYA

LAND PLANTS
475 MYA

FISH
500 MYA

REPTILES
300 MYA

MODERN HUMANS
200,000 YEARS AGO

MAMMALS
200 MYA

DINOSAURS
DIED OUT
65 MYA

SIMPLE
ANIMALS
**600 MILLION
YEARS AGO
(MYA)**

DINOSAURS
245 MYA

FLOWERS
130 MYA

TODAY

UNDER THREAT

Today, many plant and animal species are threatened by the actions of one creature – humans. With their ability to change and destroy habitats, humans are pushing many species to extinction.

20%

The IUCN (International Union for Conservation of Nature) Red List from 2008 shows that about 1,140 of the 5,500 mammal species, or 20 per cent, are threatened with extinction.

DEFORESTATION

At its peak in 1995, 29,000 square kilometres of the Amazon rainforest were being destroyed in a year – that's a rate of

3.3 SQ KM
AN HOUR

or 80 square kilometres a day, which is bigger than the island of Manhattan, New York.

WHALE DECLINE

The pre-whaling population of the blue whale was thought to be

350,000

Today there are
8–14,000

That's a fall of around
97%

SAVE THE TIGER

Figures from 2011 show an increase in the tiger population from 1,411 in 2007 to 1,706. This rise is due to the protection of the tigers' core habitats.

2007
1,411

2011
1,706

BORNEO DEFORESTATION

The area covered by rainforest on the island of Borneo (shown in green)

1950

2010

ELEPHANT DECLINE

Elephant numbers in Chad have declined from

400,000
IN 1970

TO
10,000
IN 2006

WHAT IS AN ANIMAL?

Animals are living organisms that feed on other organisms and react to the world using their senses. Found all over the world, they range in size from tiny microscopic creatures to the enormous blue whale.

THE ANIMAL KINGDOM CAN BE DIVIDED INTO TWO GROUPS:

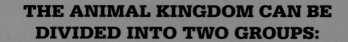

Invertebrates
animals without backbones

Invertebrates make up **95–99 per cent** of Earth's animal species.

Vertebrates
animals with backbones

MOVEMENT
While some animals live in one place, most move around in search of food and places to breed. Canada Geese can cover **2,400 km in just 24 hours** when they migrate...

... while a leatherback turtle was recorded travelling 20,558 km in 647 days.

That is the same as travelling half-way around the globe.

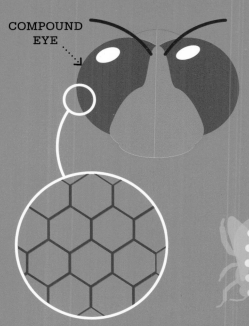

COMPOUND
EYE

Dragonflies have
as many as
30,000 lenses
in each eye.

RESPOND TO THE WORLD

Animals have special body parts that help them sense the outside world. These include eyes, ears and antennae. Insects have special compound eyes that are made up of thousands of individual units. Some animals have evolved ways of communicating, telling others about the information they have gathered.

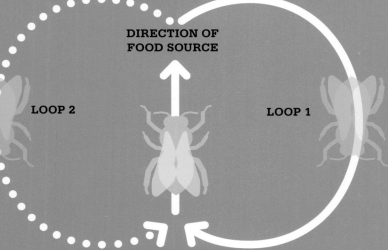

DIRECTION OF
FOOD SOURCE

LOOP 2

LOOP 1

Bees perform a **loop dance** to show others in the hive where food can be found.

EATING FOOD

Unlike plants, which can make their food using energy from the Sun, animals need to eat other living things to survive.

An adult blue whale can eat about
3.5 tonnes of krill
in a single day.

That is the same weight as three small cars.

Pythons have been recorded eating prey that is more than **50 per cent** of their own body weight.

125

CLASSIFYING ANIMALS

Scientists divide living things into groups that share the same characteristics. These groups are further divided into sub-groups, the smallest being the individual species.

KINGDOMS

The biggest groups are the kingdoms; most scientists divide the living world into **six kingdoms.** The kingdoms are divided into more and more precise sub-groups based on shared characteristics.

 ANIMALS

 PLANTS

 FUNGI

 PROTISTS
(MICRO-ORGANISMS)

 EUBACTERIA
(MICRO-ORGANISMS)

ARCHEOBACTERIA
(MICRO-ORGANISMS)

PHYLUM: *CHORDATA*
Kingdoms are divided into phyla. *Chordata* are animals that have a spinal cord.

CLASS: *MAMMALIA*
A phylum is divided into classes. Mammals are animals with hair and produce milk.

ORDER: *CARNIVORA*
A class is divided into orders. Carnivores are animals that can eat meat.

FAMILY: *FELIDAE*
An order is divided into families. *Felidae* is the family that includes the big cats.

GENUS: *PANTHERA*
A family is divided into genera (single: genus). *Panthera* includes four living species.

SPECIES: *TIGER, LION, LEOPARD, JAGUAR*
A genus is divided into different species.

HOW MANY
ANIMAL SPECIES?

Scientists have described more than **1.5 million animal species, including...**

MOTHS AND BUTTERFLIES
160,000
SPECIES

CRUSTACEANS (CRABS, LOBSTERS, ETC)
70,000
SPECIES

FISH
32,000
SPECIES

MAMMALS
6,000
SPECIES

BEETLES
400,000
SPECIES

However, it is estimated that there are around **9–10 million animal species.**

EATING AND ENERGY

The Sun is the source of most of the energy used on our planet. Plants convert this energy into substances that living things can then use to produce energy to survive and grow.

Primary consumers

Animals that eat plants are called primary consumers. They have special body adaptations to get the nutrients from plants.

A giraffe has a tongue that measures up to

50 CM

long, which it uses to grasp and pull leaves and branches off trees.

A ruminant, such as a cow, has a special stomach. This partially digests plant food, before it is regurgitated, **chewed again and swallowed**.

4. The partially digested food, now called cud, is regurgitated and chewed again.

1. Ruminant chews plant food before swallowing it.

3. The food enters the next stomach compartment, the reticulum.

5. The cud is swallowed into another part of the stomach, before going through the rest of the guts.

2. The chewed food enters the first compartment of the stomach, called the rumen.

Secondary consumers

Also known as predators, these creatures eat other animals. They have **keen senses** and **special adaptations** to hunt and catch their prey.

Some snakes use special heat-sensitive pits to hunt for prey. These pits can detect temperature variations in their surroundings of just 0.2°C.

HEAT-SENSITIVE PITS

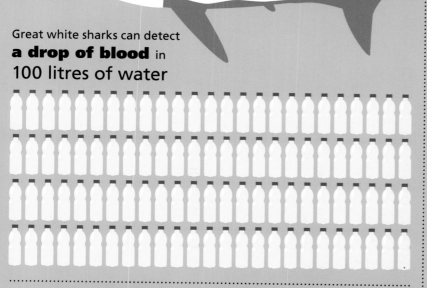

Great white sharks can detect **a drop of blood** in 100 litres of water

Sperm whales will dive to depths of around,

1,000 M

holding their breath for up to **90 minutes** while hunting for fish and squid.

THAT IS MORE THAN TWICE THE HEIGHT OF THE EMPIRE STATE BUILDING.

443.2M

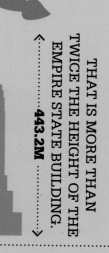

Recyclers

These creatures feed on waste and the remains of dead things.

A dung beetle can collect and bury up to **250 times** its own weight in dung in a single night.

One hectare of soil can contain **500,000 earthworms.** Together, they can eat **9 tonnes** of leaves, stems and dead roots a year (equivalent in weight to two elephants).

Earthworms range in length from **1 mm to 3 metres.**

MAMMALS

Mammals can regulate their body heat. They have bodies that are covered with hair and they feed their young on milk. Most of them give birth to live young.

YOUNG

The young of most mammals develop inside the body of the mother. This time is called the gestation period and varies from species to species.

Gestation periods

Golden hamster **2 weeks**

Human **9 months**

Blue whale **11 months**

African elephant **22 months**

The **largest newborn mammal** belongs to the **blue whale** – it weighs about **2.7 tonnes** at birth.

Three mammal species, all found in Australasia, lay eggs instead of giving birth to live young. They are called **monotremes** and include two species of **echidna**, also known as spiny anteaters, as well as the **platypus.**

ACTUAL SIZE

A platypus egg is about the size of a thumbnail. It hatches around 10 days after being laid.

The bill-like snout has special sensors to detect prey hiding in the mud of riverbeds.

A male platypus has venomous spurs on its back legs.

MILK PRODUCTION

The make-up of mammal milk varies, depending on where the animal lives and how fast the young need to grow. For example, some mammals live in cold regions and need thick layers of insulation, so their milk is very rich in fats.

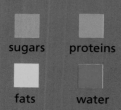

sugars proteins

fats water

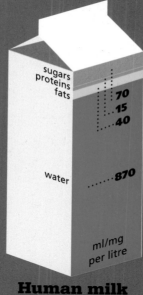

sugars
proteins
fats
70
15
40

water *870*

ml/mg
per litre

Human milk

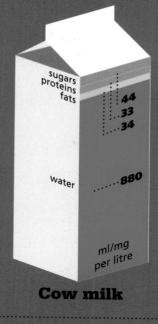

sugars
proteins
fats
44
33
34

water *880*

ml/mg
per litre

Cow milk

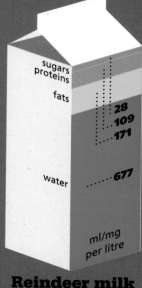

sugars
proteins

fats
28
109
171

water *677*

ml/mg
per litre

Reindeer milk

smallest and largest

ACTUAL SIZE

Kitti's hog-nosed bat
30–40 mm, 1.5–2 g

←⋯⋯ **22.5 m** ⋯⋯→

Blue whale
20–30 metres,
100–160 tonnes

MAMMAL BRAINS

Mammals usually have bigger brains than other animals of the same size.

Sperm whales have the largest brain of any living animal.

8,000 cubic cm

1,300 cubic cm

REPTILES

There are more than 9,400 species of reptile and they live on every continent, except for Antarctica. While most have four legs, some, including snakes, have no legs and slither over the ground.

Reptile characteristics

They have scales covering their bodies.

Reptiles have backbones.

They breathe air using lungs.

Most lay eggs with leathery shells.

Almost all of them are cold-blooded.

Leatherback turtles can control their body heat to a certain degree, to cope with diving into deep, icy water.

Because reptiles do not need energy to keep their **body temperature** constant, they only need to eat **2–3%** of the amount mammals and birds of similar sizes eat.

Saltwater crocodiles can lay more than 60 eggs inside a single nest.

HOW SNAKES MOVE

Snakes use different methods of pushing their bodies along the ground.

CONCERTINA

SERPENTINE

SIDEWINDING

Giant reptiles

The record for a leatherback turtle is **2.6 m long** and a weight of **916 kg.**

The Komodo dragon, the world's biggest lizard, can grow to **3 metres long** and weigh **135 kg.**

The largest living reptile is the **saltwater crocodile**, which can grow to **7 metres long** and weigh **1,000 kg...**

...as much as a small car.

AMPHIBIANS

There are about 6,500 species of amphibians found in the world. These animals cannot control their own body heat and are known as cold-blooded. They rely on the Sun to warm them up.

AMPHIBIANS WORLDWIDE

Amphibians spend their lives both in water and on dry land, and are found on every continent apart from Antarctica.

■ Inhabited by amphibians

They have no scales and their skin is permeable.

Many amphibians, like this newt, can actually 'breathe' through their skin – as a result they lose a lot of water and must spend a lot of time in water or moist places.

Amphibian metamorphosis

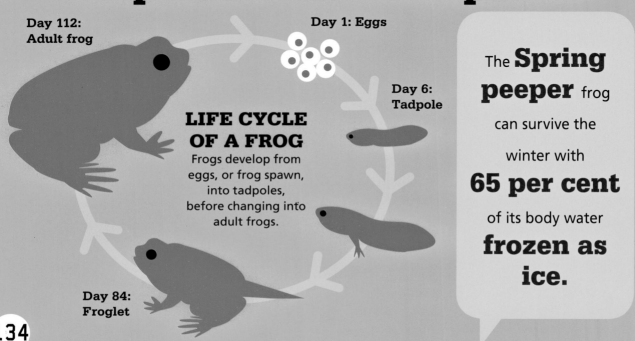

Day 112: Adult frog

Day 1: Eggs

Day 6: Tadpole

LIFE CYCLE OF A FROG
Frogs develop from eggs, or frog spawn, into tadpoles, before changing into adult frogs.

Day 84: Froglet

The **Spring peeper** frog can survive the winter with **65 per cent** of its body water **frozen as ice.**

Wallace's flying frog can glide for 15 metres or more from tree to tree (or to the ground) in search of prey or when escaping from a predator.

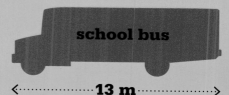

school bus

←····· 13 m ·····→

The toxins from one poison dart frog, *Phyllobates terribilis*, could kill more than

90
people.

Smallest and biggest

ACTUAL SIZE

The smallest frog in the world is found in Papua New Guinea and measures about 7.5 mm long when fully grown.

Japanese salamanders are some of the biggest amphibians in the world. They can grow to a length of 1.5 m and weigh up to **25 kg**. The biggest amphibians are **Chinese salamanders**, which can reach

1.8 m long.

BIRDS

There are more than 9,500 species of bird and they all have wings, lay eggs and have bodies that are covered with feathers. They either live in huge flocks or as solitary hunters with razor-sharp beaks and claws.

WINGS

The shape of a bird's wings depends on the type of flying it does, whether it is soaring or zig-zagging in short bursts.

ELLIPTICAL WINGS

These wings are found on birds that fly using short bursts of speed, such as robins.

ACTIVE SOARING

Long thin wings allow albatrosses to soar for a long time.

HIGH-SPEED WINGS

These are long and thin, but not as long as active soaring wings. They allow birds, such as swallows, to fly very quickly.

PASSIVE SOARING

Buzzards have wings with long, spread out feathers, which they use to catch rising currents of warm air, called thermals.

TALONS

The most powerful bird of prey, the Harpy Eagle has a wingspan of around 2 m. It talons, shown here at actual size, can be up to 12.5 cm long.

FEATHERS

All birds have feathers. They are used for insulation, to aid flying and to create amazing patterns, which birds use for display.

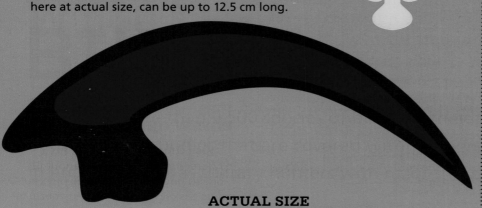

ACTUAL SIZE

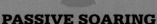

CN TOWER 553.33 M

20 mins

DIVING BIRDS

Emperor penguins can dive down to depths of **550 metres** (deeper than any other bird) and stay underwater for 20 minutes.

1,500,000,000

the number of **Red-billed Quelea** in Africa.

They form huge flocks that can take five hours to pass overhead.

LAYING EGGS

The kiwi lays the largest eggs relative to the size of its body. One female weighing 1.7 kg laid an egg weighing 0.4 kg.

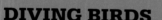

The smallest bird egg was laid by a German crested canary. It measured just 7 mm long and weighed less than 0.03 g.

ACTUAL SIZE

SMALLEST EGG

The tail of a **peacock** measures about **1.5 metres**, making up about **60%** of the bird's entire length.

FISH

There are more than 30,000 species of fish living in the salty waters of the seas and oceans and the freshwater of rivers and lakes.

Fish characteristics

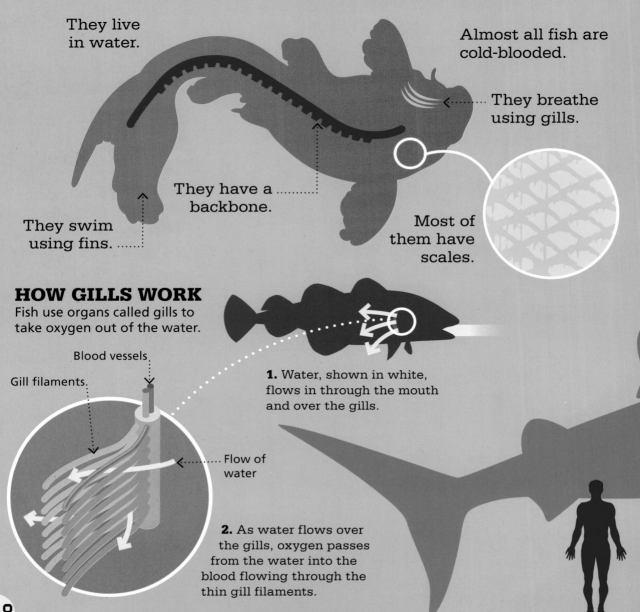

They live in water.

Almost all fish are cold-blooded.

They breathe using gills.

They have a backbone.

They swim using fins.

Most of them have scales.

HOW GILLS WORK
Fish use organs called gills to take oxygen out of the water.

Blood vessels

Gill filaments

Flow of water

1. Water, shown in white, flows in through the mouth and over the gills.

2. As water flows over the gills, oxygen passes from the water into the blood flowing through the thin gill filaments.

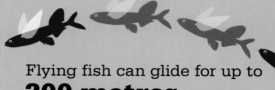

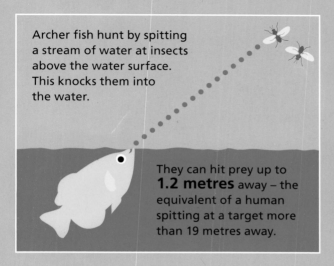

Archer fish hunt by spitting a stream of water at insects above the water surface. This knocks them into the water.

They can hit prey up to **1.2 metres** away – the equivalent of a human spitting at a target more than 19 metres away.

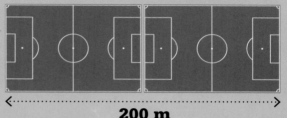

Flying fish can glide for up to **200 metres** above the water's surface – the length of two football pitches.

200 m

Record fish

Supported by water, some fish have evolved to gigantic sizes.

MOUNT EVEREST
8,848 METRES HIGH

The deepest-living fish, **Abyssobrotula galathea** was found living in a trench at the bottom of the Atlantic Ocean, some 8,370 m below the surface – almost the height of Mt Everest (8,848 m).

The world's smallest fish, *Paedocypris progenetica*, can be just **7.9 mm** long when fully grown.

ACTUAL SIZE

The biggest fish is the **whale shark.**
The largest measured specimen was **12.65 m long**.

It weighed **21 tonnes...**

... about the same as **4 elephants.**

BUGS

Insects and arachnids are part of a group of animals called arthropods. These creatures are invertebrates and are covered in hard outer skeletons called exoskeletons.

Insects and Arachnids

Insects and arachnids look **similar**, but there are key differences between the two animal **classes**.

Insects have three body parts (head, thorax and abdomen) and six legs.

Arachnids have just two body parts (cephalothorax and abdomen), but eight legs.

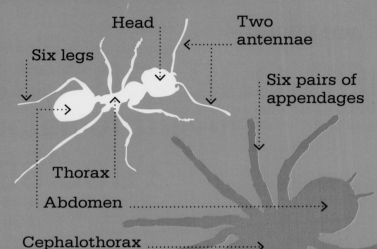

Head

Two antennae

Six legs

Six pairs of appendages

Thorax

Abdomen

Cephalothorax

Eight legs

80%

There are more species of insect than any other animal group – they make up 80 per cent of the world's arthropod species.

Insects are some of the most common living things on the planet. There are

800,000-900,000 species of insect.

Ceratopogonidae, or biting midges, can flap their wings around

1,050 times per second.

San Lorenzo forest, Panama

Many insects live in huge, hierarchical colonies.

Scientists have found as many as

25,000

species of insect living in the **6,000 hectare** San Lorenzo forest in Panama,

AN AREA SMALLER THAN MANHATTAN, NEW YORK

8,746 hectares

A termite queen can lay up to **7,000 eggs** a day, and may live for **50 years.**

A termite colony can have as many as

3,000,000

insects, including young, workers, soldiers and at least one queen.

The largest termite mound discovered measured 12.8 metres tall.

Scientists have found webs of the Darwin's bark spider in Madagascar that are **25 metres wide** – as long as two city buses.

←---- 22.5 m ----→

HARD SHELLS

Many creatures use a tough outer shell to support and protect their bodies. Even with these rigid body parts, some animals with hard shells can grow to be as big as a small car.

Types of shell

Turtle
The shell comes in two halves: the carapace on the top and the plastron on the bottom.

Crabs
As crabs grow, they continually shed and re-grow their shells, too.

Snails
A snail's shell grows along with the animal.

 # 120,000,000

The number of red crabs estimated to live on Christmas Island – 60,000 times more than the human population, which numbers just over 2,000.

ACTUAL SIZE

The largest millipede in the world is the **African giant black millipede,**

The **Japanese spider crab** can measure **3.7 m** from the tip of one claw to the other, but their bodies only measure 35 cm across.

Just 30 cm long, the **Mantis shrimp** uses a fast punch to disable prey.

Giant clams can grow to 1.2 metres across and weigh more than 225 kg – that is the weight of about **three adult humans**.

It hits with the force of a **.22 calibre bullet**, smashing through any protective shell.

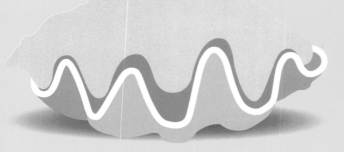

‹········· **1.2 m** ·········›

A SINGLE GARDEN SNAIL CAN HAVE **430** OFFSPRING IN A YEAR.

which can grow to nearly **40 cm long.**

OFT BODIES

s of animal species do not have a skeleton of any kind,
r external. Instead, their bodies are soft, allowing them to
through tiny gaps, or if they are supported by water, to grow
ous size.

Squid are the fastest marine invertebrates.
They squeeze out a jet of water to push
them forwards at speeds of up to

40 km/h

– faster than an Olympic
sprinter at 37.5 km/h.

Some slugs can stretch their bodies to more than **10 times**
their original length to squeeze through tiny spaces.

J KHALIFA, 829.84 M

1,000 M

Sea cucumbers live on the ocean floor at
depths ranging from 500 m to 5,000 m.
They can swim **1,000 m** up from the sea
floor while hunting for food – **higher than
the world's tallest building, the Burj**

With enormous, stinging tentacles stretching far out into the ocean, the lion's mane jellyfish is one of the world's longest creatures. The longest specimen ever found measured 37 m – longer than a blue whale.

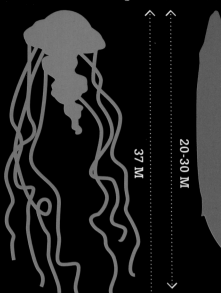

37 M

20-30 M

Giant Pacific octopuses can grow to more than **9 metres** across and weigh up to **270 kg**...

... but this is dwarfed by the monster of the deep, the giant squid, which can grow to **18 metres long** and weigh **900 kg**.

Living between **600 m** and **900 m** below the surface, the giant squid is longer than the world's biggest fish and even most whales.

ACTUAL SIZE

Giant squid have the largest eyes on the planet – up to

25 cm
in diameter

MOVERS AND SHAKERS

Some animals travel thousands of kilometres searching for water, food or the right place to raise their young. These long journeys are called migrations.

MIGRATIONS
Comparison of some of the longest migrations:

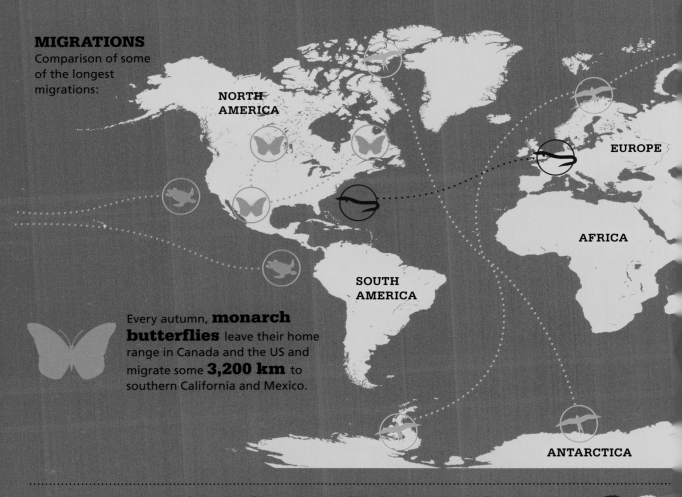

NORTH AMERICA

EUROPE

AFRICA

SOUTH AMERICA

ANTARCTICA

Every autumn, **monarch butterflies** leave their home range in Canada and the US and migrate some **3,200 km** to southern California and Mexico.

Each year, on Africa's Serengeti Plains, more than **1.5 million** wildebeest migrate in search of food. They are preyed upon by 3,000 lions.

Swarms of locusts migrate from one area when food becomes scarce. These swarms can number

10,000,000,000

and cover an area of
1,000 sq km,
around the size of Berlin, Germany's capital city.

ASIA

AUSTRALIA

European eels reproduce in the Sargasso Sea (western Atlantic and Caribbean). When the eggs hatch, the young are carried by ocean currents back to Europe, where they swim up rivers to grow and mature for up to 20 years. When fully grown they make the return trip to the Sargasso Sea to reproduce, a trip of **5,000–7,000 km** each way.

Some **Leatherback turtles** migrate **6,000 km** each way between feeding and breeding areas.

Arctic terns make a round-trip of **44,000 km** from the Arctic to Antarctica and back every year.

147

ENDANGERED AND EXTINCT

Animal species are threatened by many natural causes. But thousands of species are threatened today by the actions of humans, through hunting or habitat destruction.

90%

More than 90% of all the organisms that have ever lived on Earth are extinct.

Possible causes of extinction events:

 Gradual change in environment (cooling or warming)

 Cataclysmic event: volcanic eruption or meteorite collision

 Human activity

Mass extinction events

The **Permian mass extinction** about **250 million years ago** saw **96 per cent** of species die out, possibly because of an asteroid impact, volcanic eruptions or a drop in oxygen level – or a combination of these.

96%

↑
⋮..... survived

32.4% threatened

Of the 6,260 amphibian species listed by the IUCN (International Union for the Conservation of Nature), nearly one-third (2,030 species) are extinct or threatened.

Whaling

Blue whales are currently at one per cent of their original numbers.

1%

Humpback whales

Scientific estimates put the number of humpback whales at 1.5 million before the start of commercial whaling in the 1800s. Today, they number just

20,000

Habitat destruction

Because the forests they live in are being destroyed, scientists estimate that there are just **1,300 pandas left** in the wild. That is one panda for every 5.4 million people.

Hunting

The dodo was a flightless bird that lived on the island of Mauritius. It was first seen in 1507. Due to hunting and the introduction of predators, it was extinct by 1681.

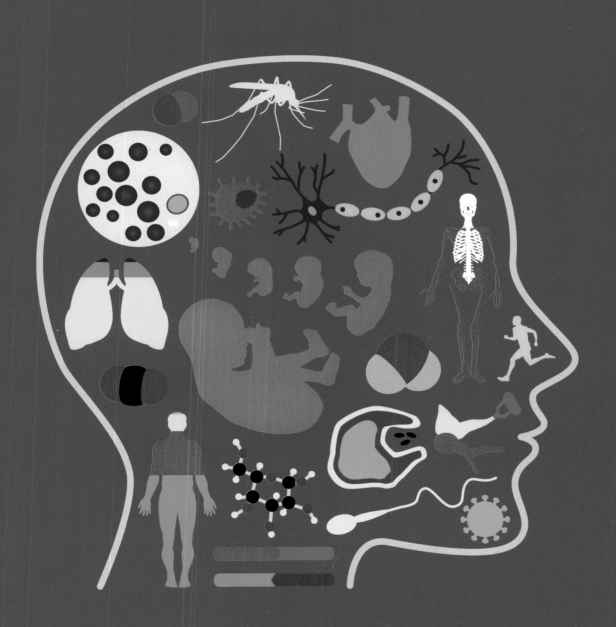

BUILDING A BODY

The human body is an amazing mixture of tiny structures called cells and a whole host of chemical substances. These cells and substances combine to form a living human being.

CELL SHAPES

Cells are microscopic structures that join together to form larger parts of the human body. Each type of cell is specially shaped to perform a job. Red blood cells are doughnut-shaped so they can carry a lot of oxygen. Sperm cells have long tails so they can swim. Nerve cells are long and thin and have branches to form a network to send messages.

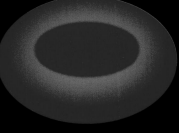

RED BLOOD CELL

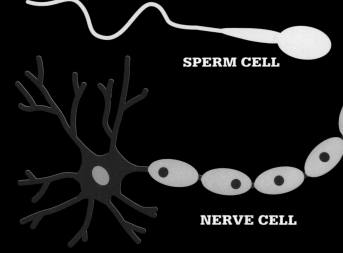

SPERM CELL

NERVE CELL

Number of cells in the body

100,000,000,000,000

3,000,000,000 cells die every minute (most of these are replaced).

1.4% NITROGEN

9.5% CARBON

A BODY CONTAINS...

ENOUGH PHOSPHORUS TO MAKE

220

MATCHES

ENOUGH FAT FOR

75

CANDLES

25.5% OXYGEN

ENOUGH CARBON TO FILL 900 **PENCILS**

ENOUGH IRON TO MAKE A NAIL THAT'S 7 CM LONG

63% HYDROGEN

HOW THE BODY IS STRUCTURED

Similar types of cell are joined together to form structures called tissues. Different tissues are joined together to create organs and these are linked to create whole body systems.

NERVE CELL

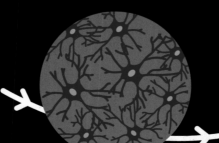

NERVE TISSUE

BRAIN

NERVOUS SYSTEM

TINY AMOUNTS OF **CALCIUM, PHOSPHORUS AND POTASSIUM**

BONE STRUCTURE

The human body keeps its shape thanks to the skeleton, a system of bones that are connected by joints.

SKELETON

The skeleton features a central part called the axial skeleton, made up of the skull, spine and ribs. Off these hang the bones of the limbs, which make up the appendicular skeleton.

A NEWBORN BABY HAS 270 BONES. MANY OF THESE FUSE TOGETHER AND BY ADULTHOOD THERE ARE 206

BONES MAKE UP ABOUT 20% OF BODY WEIGHT

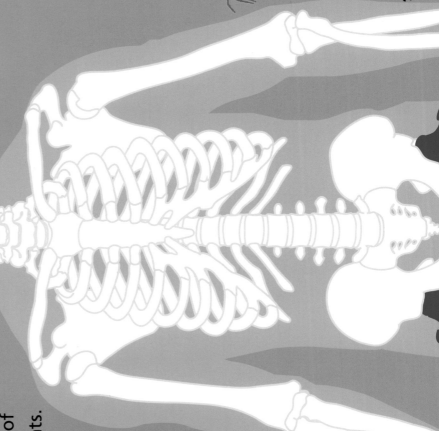

126 APPENDICULAR BONES

80 AXIAL BONES

HEALING BONES

Bone tissue has the amazing ability to repair itself when damaged. The process can take as little as a few weeks.

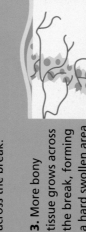

1. Just after the bone breaks, a swelling filled with clotted blood forms around it.

2. Inside the swelling, blood vessels and thin rods of bone start to grow across the break.

3. More bony tissue grows across the break, forming a hard swollen area called a callus.

4. Bone tissue grows across to heal the break.

FEMUR

FEMUR

ACTUAL SIZE

STAPES

INCUS

MALLEUS

SMALLEST BONES

Found inside the ears, these tiny bones vibrate and carry sounds to the inner ear.

LONGEST BONE

The longest bone in the body is the upper leg bone, or femur. It runs from the hip down to the top of the knee.

50 CM

155

THERE ARE ABOUT
640
SKELETAL MUSCLES, MAKING UP ABOUT
40%
OF YOUR BODY WEIGHT.

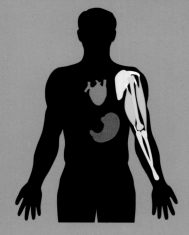

MUSCLES

All the movements that happen in your body, from lifting a leg to raising a smile, are all down to a type of tissue that can contract, called muscle.

MUSCLE TYPES

There are three types of muscle in the body: skeletal, smooth and cardiac. Skeletal muscles move the skeleton, smooth muscles perform a range of tasks, including pushing food through the gut, and the cardiac muscle powers the heart.

MUSCLE FIBRES

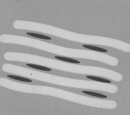

SKELETAL　　　**SMOOTH**　　　**CARDIAC**

HOW MUSCLES CONTRACT

Muscles are made up of two types of tiny muscle filament: thick and thin. These tiny muscle filaments slide over each other to make the muscle shorter.

RELAXED MUSCLE

CONTRACTING MUSCLE

FULLY CONTRACTED MUSCLE

THIN FILAMENTS

THICK FILAMENTS

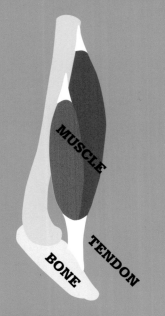

MUSCLE

TENDON

BONE

TENDONS

Skeletal muscles are attached to the bones by thick cords called tendons. The joints themselves are held together by different cords, known as ligaments.

WORKING IN PAIRS

Muscles only exert a force by contracting. This means that they can pull, but cannot push. They need to work in pairs in order to move a body part back and forth. Muscles that work together like this are called antagonistic pairs.

TENDON

BICEPS CONTRACTED

TRICEPS CONTRACTED ....▷

◁........ **BICEPS RELAXED**

TRICEPS RELAXED

TENDON

GLUTEUS MAXIMUS

The name of the largest muscle in the body, found in each buttock.

The **27** bones in your **hand** are controlled by tendons and more than **30** muscles located in the **hand** and **forearm.**

HOW MUCH CAN A MUSCLE MOVE ?

It can be shortened to
85%
CONTRACTED

RELAXED

and stretched to **120%** of its relaxed length.

STRETCHED

157

ON THE SURFACE

The outside of your body is covered with skin, hair and nails. The skin forms a protective layer, while hair keeps some body parts warm and nails help you to grip objects.

SWEAT GLANDS

Your skin is covered with up to

4 MILLION

sweat glands. The greatest concentrations are found on the palms and the soles where there are up to

350
PER SQ CM.

1 CM

1 CM

SKIN

The largest organ in the human body is the skin. New skin cells form at the bottom of the skin's outer layer. They then move to the surface, die and harden, before flaking off and being replaced.

THERE'S ENOUGH SKIN ON AN ADULT HUMAN TO COVER ABOUT

2
square
metres

SKIN MAKES UP ABOUT 12% OF YOUR BODY WEIGHT

THAT'S ABOUT

9 KG

IN A 75 KG ADULT

YOU LOSE ABOUT

50,000

flakes of dead skin every minute. That's

18 KG

HAIR CAN GROW ABOUT 0.5 MM A DAY. THAT'S 15 MM IN A MONTH.

15 MM

100,000

THE AVERAGE NUMBER OF HAIRS ON THE HUMAN HEAD.

HAIR

The shape of a person's hair is decided by the shape of the hair's cross-section.

STRAIGHT

WAVY

CURLY

AN ADULT WILL SWEAT ABOUT 0.5 LITRES PER DAY

NAILS

The hard substance that makes up nails is called keratin. It is also found in skin cells and in hair.

CHRISTINE WALTON OF THE USA HAS FINGERNAILS ON BOTH HANDS THAT MEASURE

602 CM

LONG IN TOTAL – THREE TIMES LONGER THAN A VERY TALL PERSON!

BREATHE IN, BREATHE OUT

Oxygen in the air is vital for life. Two sacs, called lungs, inside your chest take oxygen out of the air every time you breathe in.

BREATHING RATES

EXERCISING
80
BREATHS PER MINUTE

RESTING
15
BREATHS PER MINUTE

11,000
The number of litres a person will breathe on average each day.

LUNGS HAVE ABOUT
2,400 KM
OF AIRWAYS INSIDE THEM. THAT'S THE DISTANCE FROM LONDON TO ATHENS.

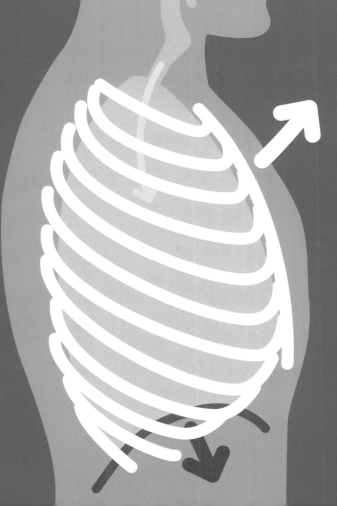

INHALE
The diaphragm contracts and flattens and the muscles between the ribs contract, pulling the ribcage up and out. This draws air into the lungs, through the tubes called airways.

THE SURFACE AREA INSIDE THE LUNGS IS

70 SQUARE METRES.

THAT'S THE SAME AS HALF A TENNIS COURT.

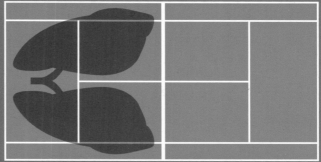

THIS LARGE AREA IS CREATED BY UP TO

500,000,000

TINY SAC STRUCTURES, CALLED ALVEOLI.

EXHALE

Air flows through the airways until it reaches the alveoli, which are surrounded by tiny blood vessels. The diaphragm and the muscles between the ribs then relax, squeezing air out of the lungs.

ALVEOLI

When air reaches the alveoli, oxygen travels into the blood vessels, while carbon dioxide passes the other way.

WHAT'S IN THE AIR WE BREATHE?

INHALED
79% Nitrogen
20% Oxygen
0.04% CO_2
Tiny amounts of water vapour and various gases

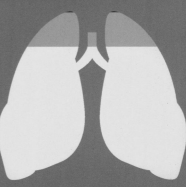

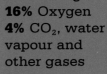

EXHALED
79% Nitrogen
16% Oxygen
4% CO_2, water vapour and other gases

EATING

Running from the mouth to the anus is a long passageway. Its role is to break down the food you eat and take out all the nutrients your body needs to operate, grow and repair itself.

YOUR MOUTH WILL PRODUCE NEARLY
40,000 LITRES
OF SALIVA IN A LIFETIME.

THAT'S ABOUT 1–1.5 LITRES EVERY DAY – EQUIVALENT TO SIX GLASSES.

9 METRES
THE LENGTH OF THE ENTIRE DIGESTIVE SYSTEM FROM MOUTH TO ANUS IF STRETCHED OUT STRAIGHT.

MOUTH

FOOD IS CHEWED INSIDE THE MOUTH.

6–10 SECONDS

OESOPHAGUS

1–4 HOURS

THE STOMACH CHURNS AND BREAKS DOWN FOOD TO FORM A MUSH.

STOMACH

LARGE INTESTINE

SMALL INTESTINE

ANUS

4 HOURS

2 HOURS

14 HOURS

YOUR INTESTINES PRODUCE ABOUT 2 LITRES OF GAS EVERY DAY.

THE SMALL INTESTINE ABSORBS MOST OF THE NUTRIENTS.

An adult will produce up to **0.25 KG OF POO A DAY.**

WHAT'S POO MADE OF? 75% WATER, 25% SOLID MATTER.

Of the solid matter, **30%** is dead bacteria, **30%** indigestible material (such as cellulose), **10–20%** cholesterol and other fats, **10–20%** inorganic substances (such as calcium phosphate), and **2–3%** proteins.

TEETH
The teeth are covered in a tough substance called enamel, which is the hardest material in the body. Each tooth is shaped to perform a specific job.

MOLAR
GRINDING AND CHEWING

PREMOLAR
GRINDING AND CHEWING

CANINE
PIERCING AND HOLDING

INCISOR
SLICING AND TEARING

PERISTALSIS
Food is pushed through the gut by waves of muscle contractions, called peristalsis.

163

BLOOD AND THE HEART

THE HEART PUMPS ABOUT 13,640 LITRES OF BLOOD AROUND THE BODY EVERY DAY.

Blood carries oxygen from the lungs and nutrients from the gut to every cell in the body. Here, they are used to produce energy and to repair damaged cells.

HOW MUCH BLOOD?

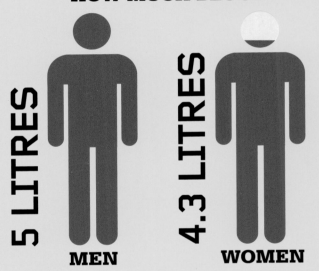

5 LITRES
MEN

4.3 LITRES
WOMEN

WHAT'S IN BLOOD?

Blood is made up of three types of blood cell; red, white and platelets. They all float about in a straw-coloured liquid called plasma.

54.3%
PLASMA

0.7% WHITE CELLS AND PLATELETS

45%
RED BLOOD CELLS

YOUR BLOOD CONTAINS UP TO

30,000,000,000

RED BLOOD CELLS.

UP TO

2,000,000

ARE MADE EVERY SECOND.

THE HEART

At the heart of the blood system is the heart! This squeezes rhythmically to push blood through the network of tubes, called blood vessels. Each heart beat has four phases.

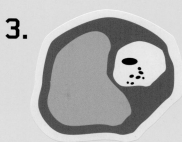

THE HEART WILL AVERAGE 70 BEATS PER MIN – ABOUT 100,000 BEATS PER DAY.

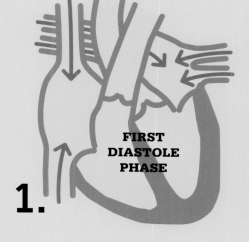

FIRST DIASTOLE PHASE

1.

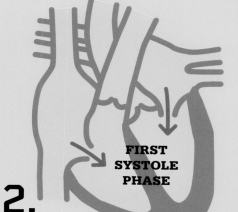

FIRST SYSTOLE PHASE

2.

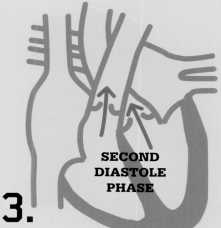

SECOND DIASTOLE PHASE

3.

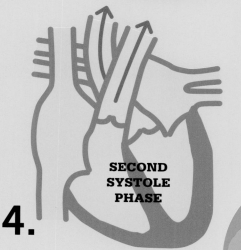

SECOND SYSTOLE PHASE

4.

AN ADULT WILL HAVE UP TO 100,000 KM OF BLOOD VESSELS – ENOUGH TO STRETCH AROUND THE WORLD 2.5 TIMES.

DEFENDING THE BODY

White blood cells help to defend the body from infection and disease. Some of them 'eat up' foreign invaders in a process called phagocytosis.

1.

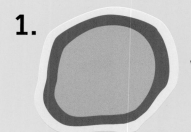

THE CELL SENSES BACTERIA NEARBY AND MOVES TOWARDS THEM

2.

THE CELL WRAPS ITS CELL MEMBRANE AROUND THE BACTERIA

3.

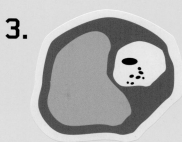

THE CELL DIGESTS THE BACTERIA

THE SENSES

Sense organs all over your body detect changes in the world around you and send signals to the brain. The organs detect pressure, heat, colours, lights, sounds, tastes and smells.

RANGE OF AUDIBLE SOUND FREQUENCIES IN HERTZ (HZ)

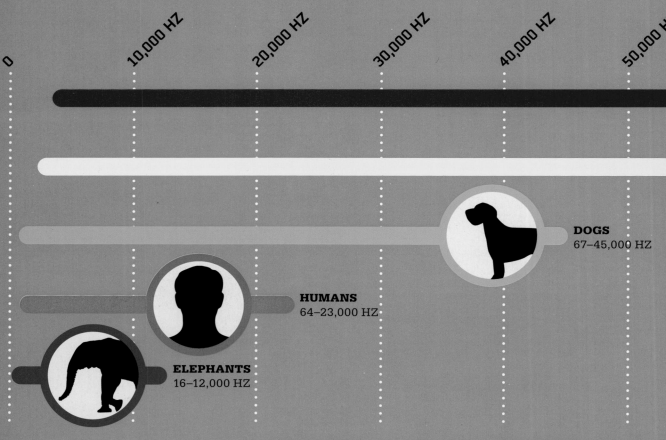

0   10,000 HZ   20,000 HZ   30,000 HZ   40,000 HZ   50,000 HZ

DOGS
67–45,000 HZ

HUMANS
64–23,000 HZ

ELEPHANTS
16–12,000 HZ

THE RETINA

The back of the eye is called the retina. It is covered with millions of special cells called rods and cones. Rods detect black and white in low light, while cones can detect all colours in bright light.

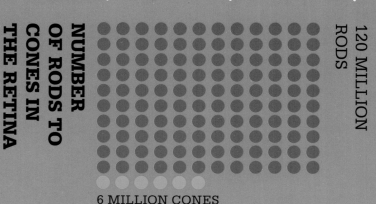

NUMBER OF RODS TO CONES IN THE RETINA

120 MILLION RODS

6 MILLION CONES

Your **nose** contains **10–20 million** smell receptor cells and these can detect more than **3,500** different odours.

60,000 HZ

70,000 HZ

80,000 HZ

90,000 HZ

100,000 HZ

BATS
2,000–110,000 HZ

MICE
1,000–91,000 HZ

HOW SENSITIVE?

Your skin is packed with touch receptors. These receptors send signals along the nervous system to a part of the brain called the sensory area. Some body parts have more touch receptors than others. This figure shows what you would look like if your body was shaped according to how sensitive each body part was, with the more sensitive parts being the biggest.

YOUR

TONGUE, LIPS AND FINGERS

WOULD BE YOUR BIGGEST PARTS,

WHILE YOUR neck and back WOULD BE VERY SMALL.

NERVOUS SYSTEM

Running through your body is a network of nerve fibres. At the centre of this network is the brain, which receives information from your senses and tells the body how to react.

THE BRAIN CONTAINS
1,000,000,000,000
NERVE CELLS

IRONED OUT FLAT, THE OUTER LAYER OF THE BRAIN WOULD COVER
2,090 SQ CM
ABOUT THE AREA OF THREE TENNIS RACKET HEADS

PRIMARY MOTOR AREA
CONTROLS VOLUNTARY MOVEMENTS

ANTERIOR SPEECH AREA
INVOLVED IN PRODUCING SPEECH

SECONDARY MOTOR AREA AND SENSORY AREA
HELPS TO COORDINATE MOVEMENTS

BRAIN GROWTH

INFANT
350 g

1 YEAR
1 KG

PUBERTY
1.3 KG

ADULT
1.5 KG

PRIMARY SENSORY AREA
PROCESSES INFORMATION
ABOUT TOUCH

300 KM/H

THE SPEED OF A NERVE SIGNAL

This is the speed of a bullet train. It takes about 0.02 seconds for a signal to travel from your foot to your brain.

POSTERIOR SPEECH AREA
ALLOWS US TO UNDERSTAND
SPEECH AND WRITING

SECONDARY VISUAL AREA
DETECTS COMPLEX
VISUAL IMAGES

PRIMARY VISUAL AREA
DETECTS SIMPLE
VISUAL IMAGES

SECONDARY AUDITORY AREA
RECOGNISES MUSIC

PRIMARY AUDITORY AREA
PROCESSES SOUNDS
FROM OUR EARS

MOTOR AREA

Each body part is controlled by a section of the primary motor area – the larger the section, the more control the brain has over that body part. This figure shows what a person would look like if their body parts were sized in relation to their section of the primary motor area.

2%

THE BRAIN MAKES UP JUST 2 PER CENT OF THE WEIGHT OF A HUMAN BODY.

THE HUMAN HOME

You are not alone! The human body is home to billions of other living organisms, from tiny bacteria to long tapeworms. Some are harmful, but many are essential to your health.

BACTERIA FOUND INSIDE THE GUT OUTNUMBER HUMAN BODY CELLS

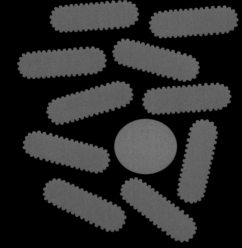

HEAD LICE

Head lice are about 3 mm long and feed by biting the scalp and sucking blood through the wound.

 <····· **ACTUAL SIZE**

MALARIA

One of the deadliest diseases, malaria, is caused by Plasmodium parasites in the blood. These parasites are carried by mosquitoes.

10 TO 1

These trillions of bacteria help to break down the chemicals in your food into simpler substances, which you can absorb into your body.

MORE THAN
750,000

PEOPLE DIE FROM MALARIA EVERY YEAR AROUND THE WORLD.

YOUR SKIN IS HOME TO ABOUT **1,000** DIFFERENT SPECIES OF BACTERIA.

600 different species of bacteria live inside a human mouth.

The beef tapeworm can grow up to

12 METRES

long inside the human intestine, the equivalent to the height of seven average-sized adult humans.

It is thought that there are **500–1,000** different **species** of **bacteria** living in the human **intestine.**

TAPEWORM EGGS HAVE BEEN FOUND IN EGYPTIAN MUMMIES, DATING FROM

2000 BCE

REPRODUCTION

To create a new human being, two tiny cells – a sperm cell from the father and an egg cell (ovum) from the mother – have to meet and fuse together. To do this, the sperm cells need to travel through the uterus and into the correct Fallopian tube.

300,000,000
RELEASED ON AVERAGE AT EJACULATION

NUMBER OF SPERM AT VARIOUS STAGES OF THE JOURNEY TO FERTILISATION

10,000
ENTER THE UTERUS

3,000 REACH THE TOP OF THE UTERUS

1,500 ENTER THE CORRECT FALLOPIAN TUBE

300 REACH THE OVUM

1 FERTILIZES THE OVUM

RELEASING EGGS

A woman is born with a huge number of egg cells, but only a small proportion of these will develop. Just one is released each month to be fertilised by sperm from a man.

500
START TO DEVELOP AT PUBERTY

1 RELEASED EVERY 28 DAYS

750,000 EGG CELLS PRESENT AT BIRTH

FUSING

Once a sperm reaches the egg cell, it burrows through the egg's outer layers and fuses with the egg.

SPERM

EGG

CELL NUCLEUS

SPERM BURROWS THROUGH OUTER LAYERS

55

The length in micrometres (millionths of a metre) of a human sperm. An egg cell is 120 micrometres across.

GROWING

Soon after fertilisation, the cell starts to divide and form a body. After some time, the cells begin to specialise, creating different body parts, such as fingers and eyes.

35 DAYS

45 DAYS

49 DAYS

56 DAYS

70 DAYS

105 DAYS

GROWING UP

A human will grow until he or she reaches a physical peak, when the body is performing at its best. This is usually at about the age of 25. After that, the body's ability to perform certain tasks starts to decline.

BODY PROPORTION CHANGES

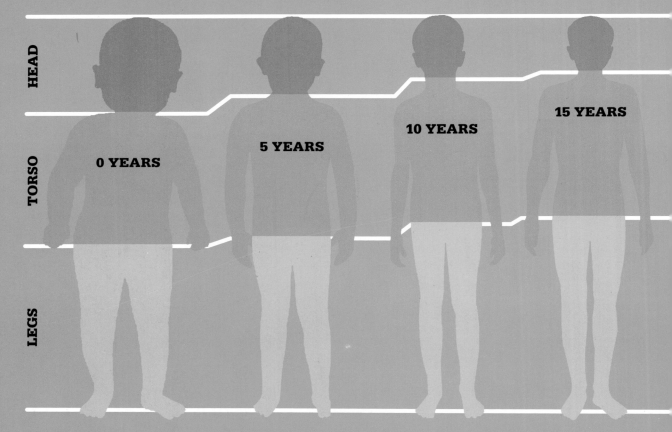

HEAD

TORSO

LEGS

0 YEARS

5 YEARS

10 YEARS

15 YEARS

GROWING BODY

People don't grow at the same rate. There are spurts of growth during puberty. These occur at the ages of about 12 for girls and 14 for boys.

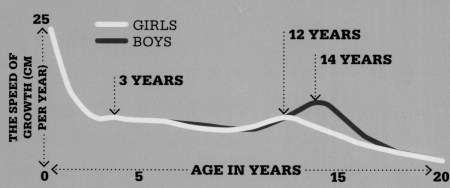

THE SPEED OF GROWTH (CM PER YEAR)

25

GIRLS
BOYS

3 YEARS

12 YEARS

14 YEARS

AGE IN YEARS

0   5   15   20

THE EFFECTS OF AGE...

MUSCLE STRENGTH

25 YEARS 100%

45 YEARS 90%

65 YEARS 75%

85 YEARS 55%

KIDNEY FUNCTION

25 YEARS 100%

45 YEARS 88%

65 YEARS 78%

85 YEARS 69%

HEAD

TORSO

LEGS

20 YEARS

BRAIN FUNCTION

25 YEARS 100%

45 YEARS 94%

65 YEARS 87%

85 YEARS 81%

LUNG CAPACITY

25 YEARS 100%

45 YEARS 82%

65 YEARS 62%

85 YEARS 50%

The **oldest** person ever was **Jeanne Calment** (1875–1997) who was **122 years** and **164 days** old when she died.

SPARE PARTS

Body parts wear out or break through injury, disease or old age. Many can be repaired, or, if the damage is serious enough, replaced with natural or artificial parts.

CORNEA
The cornea at the front of the eye can be replaced entirely or in part with a transplant from another person.

COCHLEAR IMPLANT
Also called a bionic ear, this device has microphones to collect sounds and convert them into electrical signals to send to the brain.

LUNGS
A pair of diseased lungs can be replaced with a pair donated by another person.

HEART
A human heart can be transplanted from another person or even from a pig!

PANCREAS
A pancreatic transplant may be carried out on a person suffering from diabetes. It is replaced with a pancreas from a human donor.

KIDNEY
This is the most common form of transplant, where one or both of the kidneys are replaced with kidneys from another person.

LIVER
The liver can be replaced with a whole transplant from a dead person or part of the organ from a living donor.

INTESTINE
Parts of the small or large intestine can be replaced if they have been damaged by disease.

ARTIFICIAL HIP
Metal and ceramic hip pieces replace the worn parts from the leg and hip joint.

PROSTHETIC LIMB

If an arm or leg has to be removed, or amputated, then the whole part can be replaced with a prosthetic limb. Scientists have even developed prosthetic arms and legs that can be controlled by a person's thoughts.

1967

The year of the first heart transplant. It was performed by Christian Barnard at a hospital in Cape Town, South Africa.

2011

The year of the first double leg transplant, performed by a team of surgeons at a hospital in Barcelona, Spain.

BLOOD VESSELS

Blood vessels can be replaced with transplants from another person, or they can be moved and grafted to replace damaged vessels elsewhere in the body.

SKIN

Skin can be taken from one part of the body and grafted to another to cover a serious wound.

TENDONS AND LIGAMENTS

These cord-like structures can be replaced with parts from elsewhere in the body or donations from other people.

BONE MARROW

This is found inside many bones and plays an important role in creating red blood cells. It can be replaced with a donation from another person.

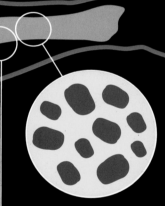

GLOSSARY

Acid rain
Rain that contains high levels of man-made pollutants. It is caused by burning fuels in factories, power stations, cars and elsewhere, and can damage buildings and the natural environment.

Adaptation
A characteristic of an animal that has come about through evolution and which gives the animal an advantage in its environment.

Amputate
To remove a body part that is diseased or badly damaged.

Appendicular skeleton
The part of the skeleton formed by the shoulders, arms, hips and legs.

Aquifer
An underground layer of rock that contains a lot of water, which can be used to supply wells.

Asexual reproduction
When something is able to create new versions of itself, or reproduce, without having to mate with another of its own species. Asexual reproduction can involve dividing or budding.

Atmospheric pressure
The force created by a planet's atmosphere pushing down onto something.

Audible
Something that can be detected by the ear. Different ranges of sound are audible to different animals.

Aurorae
Glowing patterns in the sky near to the poles. They are caused by charged particles from the Sun reacting with particles high up in the atmosphere. As well as Earth, aurorae have been spotted on other planets, including Jupiter and Saturn.

Axial skeleton
The central part of the skeleton, formed by the skull, backbone and ribs.

Bacteria
Tiny forms of life that are made up of one cell.

Big Bang
The theory that the Universe was formed by an enormous explosion and that all the matter in space was created in the first moments of this event. This matter then joined together to form stars, clouds, galaxies and planets.

Biofuel
Fuel derived from renewable natural resources, such as crops.

Organ
A group of body tissues that work together to carry out particular jobs in the body. The heart, brain, stomach and skin are all examples of organs in the human body.

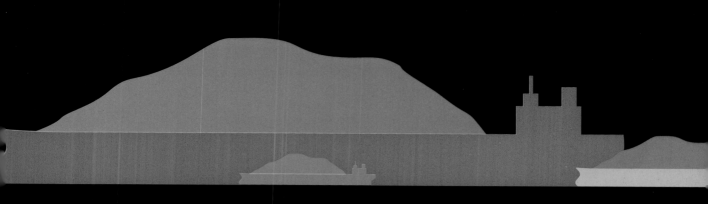

Biomass
The total amount of organisms in an area.

Blast furnace
A very hot oven for making iron in which the temperature is raised by blasts of air.

Blood vessels
Tubes that carry blood around the body. There are three kinds of blood vessel: arteries, which carry blood from the heart; capillaries, which carry blood from the arteries to individual cells in the body; and veins, which carry blood from the capillaries back to the heart.

Borehole
A tunnel drilled into the ground and often used to look for, or access, natural resources.

Cell
The fundamental building block of life. Cells are able to perform all of the functions that are essential for life, including producing energy and reproducing.

Characteristic
A feature or quality of an animal.

Coke oven
An oven for converting coal, a fuel with many impurities, into coke, a much purer fuel.

Cold-blooded
Unlike warm-blooded animals, cold-blooded animals cannot regulate their own temperature, but rely on the heat of the Sun to warm them up. Cold-blooded animals are often slow-moving in cold weather.

Consumer
An organism which feeds off other organisms that produce energy from sunlight.

Continents
Large areas of land. The Earth has seven continents: Asia, Africa, North America, South America, Europe, Australia and Antarctica.

Contract
To shorten in length. Muscles contract in order to exert a pulling force.

Core
The centre of an astronomical body, such as a planet or a star.

Core of the Earth
The mass that lies at the centre of the Earth. It is divided up into the outer core, which is 2,200 km thick, and an inner core, which has a radius of about 1,300 km.

Crude oil
Oil in its natural state before it is converted, or refined, into useful products, such as petrol.

Igneous
A type of rock that forms from the cooling of magma or lava.

Crust
The outer layer of a rocky planet. The crust is usually made up of hard rock. The Earth's crust is up to 100 km thick.

deforestation
The cutting down of large areas of forest.

Lava
When magma reaches the Earth's surface during a volcanic eruption, it is called lava.

Diaphragm
A sheet of muscle that sits across the bottom of the ribs and helps you to breathe.

DNA
Short for deoxyribonucleic acid, this is the complex, twisting molecule found inside cells. It carries the genetic information that tells the cells how to perform.

Dwarf planet
A small planet whose body is shaped by its own gravity, but is not big enough to clear its region of other astronomical bodies. Dwarf planets include Pluto, Vesta and Eris, which lie at the very edge of the Solar System.

Element
A substance that cannot be broken down into any other substances.

Equinox
A point in the Earth's orbit around the Sun when day and night are equal lengths. There are two equinoxes: in spring and autumn.

Evolution
The process by which plants and animals change and adapt to the altering conditions around them.

Evolved
Something that has changed over time – all animal species gradually change and adapt to their environments.

Exoskeleton

A hard, protective outer covering that some invertebrates have.

Extinct

Something that has died out and no longer exists.

Fossil fuel

A fuel made from the decayed remains of dead organisms. Coal and oil and are fossil fuels.

Galaxy

An enormous collection of stars that are held together by gravity. Galaxies come in many different shapes, including spiral and elliptical.

Galvanising

Covering iron or steel with a rust-resistant coating of zinc.

Genome

A term that refers to all the genetic information of an organism, including the genes.

Geothermal energy

Energy derived from the heat of the Earth's interior.

Gestation

The period between an egg being fertilised and the young being born – also known as pregnancy.

Gills

The breathing organs of fish and some other aquatic animals, which extract oxygen from the water.

Global warming

A gradual increase in the Earth's average temperature.

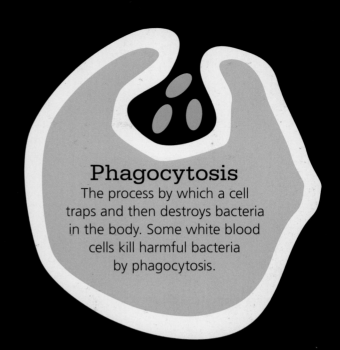

Phagocytosis

The process by which a cell traps and then destroys bacteria in the body. Some white blood cells kill harmful bacteria by phagocytosis.

Graft

To move tissue from one part of the body to another. Where a person has badly damaged skin, doctors may graft skin from another part of the body to mend the damaged area.

Gravity

The force that attracts one object to another. The amount of gravity an astronomical body has depends on its mass.

Greenhouse effect

The process by which the atmosphere traps heat given off by the Earth before it can escape into space. This trapped heat warms up the atmosphere.

Greenhouse gases

Gases, such as carbon dioxide and methane, which can trap heat in the atmosphere. This effect is similar to how the glass in a greenhouse traps the Sun's heat.

Groundwater

Water that lies beneath the Earth's surface.

Habitat
The environment in which an organism lives.

Hierarchical
A group of things that is arranged in order of importance. A hierarchical colony or society has the most important individuals at the top and the least important at the bottom.

Hydroelectric power
Electricity made by harnessing the power of flowing water.

Industrialisation
The rapid development of industries.

Invertebrate
An animal that does not have a backbone.

Keratin
A tough substance that is an important part of the skin, nails and hair.

Ligaments
Strong, cord-like tissues that connect one bone to another.

Star
A large ball of gas whose mass is so great that atoms deep inside its core are squeezed together, fusing them. This releases an enormous amount of energy, which escapes as light and heat.

Magma
Molten rock that is found beneath the Earth's surface.

Magnitude
How strong something is. For example, the magnitude of an earthquake is measured by the Richter scale – a higher reading on this scale indicates a stronger earthquake.

Mantle
The region inside the Earth that lies beneath the crust and above the core. It reaches down to a depth of 2,900 below the surface and is made up of molten rock.

Metamorphic
A type of rock that has been created extreme heat and pressure.

Metamorphosis
When an organism goes through a change in its body as it gets older. F example, a butterfly starts life as a before building a cocoon and finally as the adult butterfly.

Micro-organism
A living creature that is too small to with the naked eye.

Mineral
A naturally occuring substance mad one – or usually several – elements.

Molecule

The smallest unit of a chemical. Molecules can be very simple and made up of two atoms, such as the gas oxygen, or they can be very complex, as with DNA.

Molten

A substance that has become liquid by getting very hot. For example, the metal iron becomes molten at 1,538°C.

Monotreme

A rare type of mammal that lays eggs rather than giving birth to live young.

Moon

A natural satellite in orbit around a larger astronomical body. Moons are found around planets, dwarf planets and even asteroids. The Earth has one moon, while Jupiter has more than 60.

Muscle filament

Thin strands of muscle tissue that slide over each other when the muscle contracts.

Non-renewable

Something that can be used only once. Coal is a non-renewable fuel source.

Notochord

A simple version of the backbone. It is a flexible rod that is found in some species and in the developing young of all vertebrates (animals with backbones).

Nucleus

The structure found inside a eukaryotic cell which houses its genetic material in the form of DNA.

Orbit

The path of one object around another. For example, the planets of the Solar System follow long, oval-shaped orbits around the Sun, while the Moon orbits the Earth.

Ore

A type of mineral that contains metals.

Organism

A living thing. An organism may be large, such as a human, or tiny, such as a bacterium.

migrate

To move to a new area, usually in search of food, water, partners to mate with, or a suitable place to raise young.

Oxygen furnace

A very hot oven in which pure oxygen is blown through molten iron to make steel.

Pangaea

The name given to the enormous piece of land formed on Earth 270 million years ago.

Permeable

A permeable skin or membrane is one that allows gas or fluids to pass through it.

Photosynthesis

The process by which plants use chlorophyll to capture the energy from sunlight, turning water and carbon dioxide into sugar and oxygen.

Planet

An astronomical body that goes around or orbits a star. A planet is big enough to clear its region of other, smaller objects, but is not massive enough to start the fusion of atoms in its core, as happens in the cores of stars. There are eight planets in the Solar System.

Plasma

A straw-coloured liquid that makes up more than 50 per cent of blood. Red and white blood cells are carried in the plasma.

Pole

One of the two ends of a magnet. A magnetic pole can be either North (N) or South (S).

Precipitation

Water that falls to the ground as rain or snow.

Producer

An organism that produces energy using sunlight.

Prokaryotic cell

A type of cell that does not have a nucleus to hold its genetic information.

Puberty

A period of body development that starts at around age 12 in girls and 14 in boys. During puberty, the body grows very quickly and changes shape, and the sexual organs develop.

Radiation

A type of energy that is released in wave form, such as light, or as tiny subatomic particles.

Refined

Processed to remove the impurities and create new products. For instance, oil is refined to produce petrol.

Relaxed

A state in which muscles are not exerting a pulling force. Relaxed muscles are longer than muscles that are contracting.

Renewable

Something that can be replaced after it has been used. Wind and wave power are renewable energy sources.

Resources

Materials that can be used to produce goods or energy. These can include natural resources, such as coal, oil and minerals, and human resources, such as the size of a workforce.

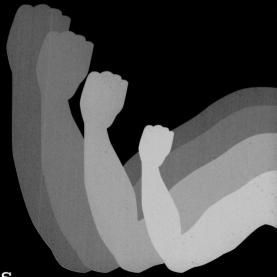

Respiration

The process by which organisms produce energy, releasing carbon dioxide and water as a result.

Retina

An area at the back of the eye that contains special cells that detect light. The retina sends information to the brain along the optic nerve.

Richter scale

The scale used to measure the strength of an earthquake – the higher the number the more powerful the tremor.

Saliva

A watery substance produced inside the mouth. Saliva contains chemicals that start the process of digestion as we chew our food.

Satellite

An astronomical object that orbits another. Moons are natural satellites and they orbit around planets. Artificial satellites are found orbiting Earth where they study space and examine the Earth's surface.

Sedimentary

A type of rock that is formed by small rock particles that have settled from water and been squashed together.

Senses

The ways in which animals gather information about the the outside world. This includes sight, hearing, smell, taste and touch, as well as several other senses.

Sexual reproduction

When two animals of the opposite sex produce young together.

Sinter

A mixture of iron ore and limestone used in the production of steel.

Solstice

A point in the Earth's orbit around the Sun when one hemisphere experiences the longest day and shortest night. There are two solstices: one in summer and the other in winter.

Species

A group of organisms that are very similar to each other and can reproduce with each other to produce fertile offspring. All living beings belong to one particular species.

Subalpine zone
A region that lies just below the tree line on the side of a mountain.

Subarctic zone
The region that lies between the Arctic and the temperate regions.

System
A group of organs in the body that work together to carry out particular jobs. One organ may work for several different body systems. For instance, the liver works for the digestive system and the circulatory system.

Taiga
A type of coniferous forest that is found in a large band south of the Arctic, running through North America, northern Europe and Russia.

Eukaryotic cell
A type of cell that contains several specific structures, including a nucleus, which holds the cell's genetic information.

Tectonic plates
The large pieces of the Earth's surface that fit together to form the crust. These pieces are crashing into each other, pulling apart or rubbing against one another.

Tendons
Strong, cord-like tissues that connect muscles to bones.

Thermal
A rising current of warm air.

Tide
The rise and fall of the Earth's oceans caused by the gravitational pull of the Moon and Sun. This pull forms a bulge in the oceans, creating high tide. The tides rise and fall twice each day as the Earth spins around.

Tissue
A group of similar cells in the body that does one particular job.

Torso
The part of the body to which the limbs and neck are attached. The torso contains most of the body's important organs.

Transpiration
When plants give off water vapour.

Uterus
Part of the female reproductive system in mammals. It is where developing young grow before birth.

Vertebrate
An animal that has a backbone.

Virus
A type of organism that can only replicate inside another living being.

Warm-blooded
Warm-blooded animals can control their own temperatures and do not need to rely on the heat of the Sun.

Watt
A unit of energy; 1,000 watts equals a kilowatt, while 1,000 kilowatts equals a megawatt.

Year
The amount of time it takes for a planet to complete one orbit around the Sun. A year on Earth takes about 365 days, and it would complete nearly 12 orbits in the time it takes Jupiter to finish one.

Websites

MORE INFO:
www.metoffice.gov.uk
Website of the UK's Meteorological Office. It contains information on current weather conditions around the world, as well as global climate patterns.

www.zsl.org
The webiste of the Zoological Society of London. It contains information on conservation and the latest scientific studies on animal life.

http://faculty.washington.edu/chudler/neurok.html
A website packed with fascinating information about the brain for kids and adults.

kids.nationalgeographic.com/kids/places/
Part of the children's section of the National Geographic website. This offers lots of information about different countries.

www.howstuffworks.com
A massive website featuring explanations of how nearly everything works, including machines and vehicles. It features videos, games and blogs.

www.nasa.gov/audience/forkids/kidsclub/flash/
The kids page of the NASA website contains fun facts, games, photos and information about space.

MORE GRAPHICS:
www.visualinformation.info
A website that contains a whole host of infographic material on subjects as diverse as natural history, science, sport and computer games.

www.coolinfographics.com
A collection of infographics and data visualisations from other online resources, magazines and newspapers.

www.dailyinfographic.com
A comprehensive collection of infographics on an enormous range of topics that is updated every single day!

INDEX

ACKNOWLEDGEMENTS

First published in 2014 by Wayland
Copyright © Wayland 2014

Wayland
338 Euston Road
London NW1 3BH

Wayland Australia
Level 17/207 Kent Street
Sydney NSW 2000

All rights reserved.

ISBN: 978 0 7502 8121 8
E-book ISBN: 978 0 7502 8827 9

Senior editor: Julia Adams

Produced by Tall Tree Ltd
Editor: Jon Richards
Designer: Ed Simkins
Consultants: John Clancy (The Human Body);
Dr Vincent Béal (The Human World);
Penny Johnson (Machines and Vehicles); Paola
Oliveri (The Natural World); John Williams
(Planet Earth); Professor Raman Prinja (Space)

A CIP catalogue record for this book is available
from the British Library.

10 9 8 7 6 5 4 3 2 1

Printed in Hong Kong

Wayland is a division of Hachette
Children's Books, an Hachette UK company.
www.hachette.co.uk

The website addresses (URLs) included in this
book were valid at the time of going to press.
However, due to the nature of the Internet, it is
possible that some addresses may have changed,
or sites may have changed or closed down, since
publication. While the author and Publisher
regret any inconvenience this may cause, no
responsibility for any such changes can be
accepted by either the author or the Publisher.